WOMEN AND WORK

WOMEN AND WORK

Twenty-five Years of Gender Equality in Wales

Teresa Rees

Published on behalf of
the Board of Celtic Studies
of the University of Wales

UNIVERSITY OF WALES PRESS • CARDIFF • 1999

British Library Cataloguing-in-Publication Data.
A catalogue record for this book is available from the British Library.

ISBN 0–7083–1495–3

Typeset at University of Wales Press
Printed in Great Britain by Gwasg Dinefwr, Llandybïe

Contents

List of figures

List of tables

Preface and acknowledgements

This book looks at women in the Welsh workforce in the period since the mid-1970s when equality legislation, designed to put an end to sex discrimination in recruitment, training and pay, was first introduced. While there has undoubtedly been progress towards equality between men and women, alas some of this is as a result of the deterioration in the position of men. Differences among women are now more apparent. The interactions between gender and other dimensions which inform the way we organize education, training and paid work, such as class, ethnic origin, the Welsh language, urban or rural location and disability, are proving complex and giving rise to new forms of inequalities.

As well as reviewing changes brought about by patterns of industrial restructuring and the increase in the numbers of women in employment over the last two decades or so, the book also provides a more detailed snapshot of the current situation. What kinds of jobs do women have, in what sectors? How many are in senior decision-making positions? How do women balance home and work lives? It concludes with some ideas for policy approaches to ameliorate the extent to which gender remains such a significant determinant of who gets what job, and with what prospects for pay, training and pension in Wales.

The material presented here will hopefully be helpful to those interested in women and gender relations generally in Wales and those concerned with education, training and the labour market more specifically. This includes students and academics but also employers, trade unions, Training and Enterprise Councils, local authorities, further and higher education providers, development and enterprise agencies, careers companies and hopefully, the new National Assembly for Wales.

The book draws upon research originally commissioned by Chwarae Teg with support from the Equal Opportunities Commission (EOC), and I am grateful to both organizations for their support. A summary of the research is available from Chwarae Teg.

I am also grateful to the Board of Celtic Studies for supporting the publication of this book through the University of Wales Press. Staff at the Press, in particular Sue Charles, Richard Houdmont and Ceinwen Jones, have as usual combined patience with persistence which ensured the completion of the manuscript.

A number of people assisted considerably with the collection of the data upon which the book draws. Dawn Snape (now at Social and Community Planning Research but then at the School for Policy Studies, University of Bristol) amassed most of the data for the tables in the appendix under the kind tutelage of Professor Martin Boddy: I am most grateful to them both for wrestling with the difficulties of charting changes over the decades despite changing categories and boundaries. Chapter 4 draws on research on women in post-compulsory education and training in Wales originally commissioned by the EOC and conducted with David Istance (now of OECD) whose input is gratefully acknowledged here: a full account of that project can be found in Istance and Rees (1995). Finally, Val Feld, the Director of the Wales Office of the EOC, Ian Willox of the Welsh Development Agency and Jane Hutt of Chwarae Teg together with members of the Research Steering Group of the EOC have kindly provided advice and support throughout the project, Jenny Capstick of the School for Policy Studies, University of Bristol, worked long, hard and cheerfully on endless amendments to text and tables and Alison Parker prepared the index.

Despite the fact that I am the current EOC Commissioner for Wales, the views expressed in this book are my own and do not necessarily represent those of the EOC.

Teresa Rees

Abbreviations

DfEE	Department for Education and Employment
EC	European Commission
EOC	Equal Opportunities Commission
EU	European Union
GB	Great Britain
GCSE	General Certificate of Secondary Education
ILO	International Labour Office
LFS	Labour Force Survey
MEP	Member of European Parliament
MEWN	Black and Ethnic Minority Women's Network
MP	Member of Parliament
NHS	National Health Service
NOMIS	National Online Manpower Information System
NOW	New Opportunities for Women
NTETs	National Training and Education Targets
NVQ	National Vocational Qualifications
OECD	Organization for Economic Co-operation and Development
SGWW	South Glamorgan Women's Workshop
SATs	Standard Assessment Tests
TEC	Training and Enterprise Council
UK	United Kingdom
WDA	Welsh Development Agency

1 Introduction

In 1970, legislation was passed in Parliament which was to prove a watershed for women in work in Britain. The Equal Pay Act and the Sex Discrimination Act, which came into effect in 1975, outlawed discrimination on the grounds of sex for hiring, firing and pay. Employers were given five years to make arrangements to comply with the legislation. The Equal Opportunities Commission (EOC) was set up as a watchdog to oversee compliance with the law, to promote equality of opportunity between men and women, and to advise the government when changes were needed in sex equality legislation. The EOC provides information and advice on equal opportunities and assists some individuals and groups who want to bring cases against employers under the legislation.

The legislation, which needed to be enacted in order to comply with European Community law, raised the level of awareness of issues related to 'equal opportunities' in the workplace, but in other respects has been muted in its effects. Women in Britain still only earn roughly 80 per cent of men's wages – although this is clearly an improvement on the 1975 figure of 71 per cent (*New Earnings Survey* 1975; 1995). They still get fired for getting pregnant or wanting to shift to part-time hours, despite its illegality and numerous high-profile victories in the courts on just these grounds. And the labour force remains rigidly divided into men's jobs and women's jobs. Equal opportunities has proved to be a highly complex concept. Legislation, while important, clearly needs to be accompanied by a shift in mind-set and attitudes as well as practices and policies. Just how has the situation changed for women in Wales over the last twenty-five years? And what are the key issues which need to be addressed now?

This book illustrates that while there is much to celebrate, there is still a considerable way to go before gender ceases to have such a significant impact on who gets what education, training, employment and pay in the Welsh workforce. Meanwhile, some employers, particularly in North America but also in the United Kingdom, the European Union and indeed elsewhere in the global economy, are increasingly recognizing that being 'smart' in the use made of human resources is crucial to profitability. We in Wales need to learn from our history and from the lessons of statistics on women in the workforce in order to avoid the low-wage/low-skill syndrome. Equal opportunities is not simply a matter of social justice: it is now widely recognized as making good business sense (Humphries and Rubery 1996).

In seeking to review the position of women in the Welsh workforce over the last twenty-five years, three main difficulties are encountered. The first of these relates to the fact that, during the early part of this period in particular, relatively few published statistics give a breakdown by sex. The situation has improved immeasurably since 1970, although there are still significant gaps (see Istance and Rees 1994 in relation to post-compulsory education and training statistics in Wales). However, to chart change over time has proved problematic. Categories have also changed over this period and of course local government boundaries have been reorganized twice over the past twenty-five years: once in 1974 and again in 1996. The figures given in what follows, therefore, include some surrogate measures. This problem is not, of course, unique to Wales and encouraging those bodies which produce statistics routinely to provide a gender breakdown is one of the EOC's current concerns.

The second difficulty relates to the lack of research on women and work in Wales over the period, especially in the first decade. The late 1980s and early 1990s saw a substantial development of interest in and research on this issue in the UK, and this is reflected in the increase of published material in Wales during that period. Moreover, general studies of the economy and the labour force are now far more likely to pay attention to gender differences. However, some research published on the Welsh economy still lacks a gender dimension and coverage is far from comprehensive. Key questions posed by the statistics remain unanswered by the research literature.

The final difficulty concerns charting differences *among* women. In some cases, dissimilarities among women in terms of their access to education, training and employment opportunities can be greater than those between women and men. However, in a small country such contrasts are rarely revealed in either statistics or studies. Hence there are relatively few sources of data on women from ethnic minorities within Wales, on particular issues faced by Welsh-speakers or the experiences of lesbian women or women who have disabilities.

The interrelationship between these dimensions is particularly hard to chart: women, like men, have multiple identities. Spatial dimensions are crucial in Wales, but boundaries used for administrative and statistical purposes do not follow neatly the contours of geographical features which so impact upon patterns of settlement and movement. The south Wales valleys, for example, confound distinctions made on an urban/rural basis and yet their geographical characteristics have profound implications for access to education, training and employment. I have sought to illustrate the similarities and differences among women of different ethnic origin, first language and geographical base as far as possible, but I am keenly aware that there are gaps in the coverage of these important dimensions: data are even more sparse on disability and sexual orientation.

This book draws upon a range of different sources. These include general studies of the Welsh economy (including some which are 'gender-blind'); 'political arithmetic' studies which look at the distribution of men and women in different industrial sectors and occupations in the labour market; case studies of women in particular jobs or sectors and small-scale action research projects on issues related to the balancing of work and home lives. While many of the sources are publicly available, some are in the form of 'grey literature' in internal reports of various organizations, and some of the tables of statistics have been especially generated from unpublished data from surveys such as the 1991 Census and the *Labour Force Survey*.[1]

Finally, it is not simply the position of women in work that has changed significantly over the last twenty-five years. Wales itself has changed beyond all recognition (see Aull Davies 1989; Herbert and Jones 1995) and is likely to undergo further transformation with the advent of the Welsh Assembly. We now have a host of Welsh institutions, such as the Welsh Development Agency, the Development Board for Rural Wales and the Land Authority for Wales (soon to merge to become the 'Economic Powerhouse' Welsh Development Agency), the Funding Councils for Further and Higher Education in Wales, the Training and Enterprise Councils and the careers service companies. New unitary authorities have been established throughout the Principality (although plans to set up such arrangements in England appear to have been abandoned). Some public sector functions have been privatized and the number of semi-autonomous government organizations has multiplied: indeed, Wales has been dubbed 'Quangoland' (Morgan and Roberts 1993). The Labour government has embarked on a programme of reducing and streamlining quangos.

From the stereotypical images of coal, steel and industrial despoliation of the 1970s, Wales in the late 1990s is characterized by reclaimed land, tourism, inward investment factories, high-tech initiatives, the growth of the service sector and new infrastructure by road, land and air. Unemployment has dropped to the level of the UK average, but this is partly related to the fact that the proportion of people outside the labour force in Wales, who are prematurely retired or chronically sick, has increased substantially. Women's employment has grown to average UK levels, but wages remain among the lowest.

The next chapter briefly chronicles some of these contextual shifts. Following chapters deal with more specific changes in employment patterns, education and training and new strategies for balancing home and work. The final chapter addresses new approaches to equal opportunities to take us into the next millennium.

2 Industrial restructuring and demographic change

Introduction

The industrial structure of Wales has changed dramatically in the last twenty-five years. From the traditional domination of coal, steel and agriculture, much of the landscape is now characterized by reclaimed land, advance factories and big manufacturing plants owned by inward investment companies from the United States, Germany and Pacific Rim countries. The development of service-sector industries in finance, insurance, tourism and leisure has generated a demand for office blocks and workers with completely different skills. Big Pit in Blaenavon is now an industrial museum where ex-miners are employed as museum guides. The 'set-aside' policy in agriculture has led to farmland in Dyfed being turned into golf courses and the 'Oakwood experience': a theme park with daring rides and adventures which is now one of the top tourist attractions in the Principality. North Wales is increasingly known for its bed-and-breakfast accommodation and its studios and production companies rather than its slate quarries and power station, while Cardiff with its redeveloped bay has become a recognized administrative and commercial capital and centre for the media and film animation. Red-brick business parks and hotels adorn the verges of both the M4 in the south and the A55 in the north and the new colour-coordinated second Severn crossing promises more business, traffic and communication with England and beyond.

There have been winners and losers in these tremendous upheavals (not least among the latter, the wading birds of the Gwent estuary). For some, the expansion of the service sector has meant job opportunities where none existed before. The growth in education and training has encouraged some to pursue qualifications that have enhanced their chances in the job market. Some employees struggle with long hours and stress, while others have to accommodate the frustration of low pay, poor rewards and a lack of recognition of their talents. Many people have become self-employed or set up their own small businesses: some were pulled towards it as an opportunity; others, such as redundant miners, felt pushed into creating their own jobs in the absence of alternatives (Rees and Thomas 1991). At the same time, long-term unemployment has become a way of life not just for some individuals but for whole families and communities, particularly in the hard-hit south Wales valleys and in the farming communities of rural Wales where suicide rates testify to the personal tragedies ensnared in processes of industrial change.

These shifts in the industrial structure are of course reflected in the nature and characteristics of the workforce. The image of the Welsh Mam of coalfield communities, encapsulated in films such as *How Green Was My Valley* and *The Corn is Green*, is clearly no longer the potent stereotype it once was (Beddoe 1986). From full-time, arduous home-based work, women in Wales are now more likely to be in paid employment themselves, half of them in part-time work in the service sector. The women's film co-operative Red Flannel Films' production of *Mam*, premièred in 1988 in Treorchy's Park and Dare Hall, was a landmark in demolishing the myth of the Welsh Mam and substituting a range of other images more accurately reflecting the diversity and complexities of women's lives in modern Wales.

The 1984/5 miners' strike acted as an effective mass consciousness-raising exercise for miners' wives in recognizing their own potential (Adler 1989). It led to initiatives such as the Dove Training Workshop for women in coal-mining communities being set up in Banwen in the Dulais Valley. The Workshop has attracted many women and men back into education and developed strong links with community initiatives in other coal-mining regions of Europe.

In 1994, *Our Sisters' Land: The Changing Identities of Women in Wales* was published. It includes a collection of 'voices' of women in Wales, illustrating a diverse range of private and public identities (Aaron et al. 1994). The voices show women as both crucially embedded in supporting their families but also involved more and more in public life, in paid work, politics, the voluntary sector, campaigns, the arts, business, education and initiatives whereby they create their own businesses and organizations.

From contributing to the economy largely in indirect and unrecognized ways in the 1970s, half the women of working age in Wales in the late 1990s are now themselves in the workforce.

Moreover, while the proportion of women who are in the workforce has increased, that of men has decreased. However, despite predictions based upon changes in the industrial structure, women have not become breadwinners. Wales remains unfortunately characterized by low-paid work for women. While the Equal Pay Act meant that from 1975 it was no longer legal to pay men and women different rates for the same work, many women in Wales today are employed in relatively low-skilled work with few prospects for training and promotion, earning considerably less than rates paid to men for 'men's jobs' (Istance and Rees 1996). Indeed, in Britain as a whole the hourly rates of women working part-time has fallen as a percentage of full-time women workers' wages (Walby 1997) and pay rates are lower in Wales than elsewhere. This is directly linked to patterns of industrial restructuring and is a key issue to be tackled in Wales for the future.

This chapter identifies some of the main elements of industrial and demographic change in Wales over the last two and a half decades. There have clearly been substantial job losses in coal and steel, although manufacturing, while in decline, remains more significant in Wales than elsewhere in the UK. It is the development of the service sector, however, that has created employment opportunities for women. Young, well-qualified women are gaining entry to the professions. However, very few reach senior managerial or decision-making positions compared with women elsewhere in Britain. Less-qualified and unqualified women find it extremely difficult to secure employment that offers training, prospects or a decent wage.

Without the provision of effective opportunities to acquire skills and qualifications later in life, combined with affordable childcare, class divisions are reproduced rather than challenged. Hence while younger women are catching up and overtaking boys in educational achievement at some levels at school, gender differences in qualifications for older groups remain marked. There are now widespread public concerns about the relatively poor educational achievement of boys, coupled with severe problems associated with long-term unemployment now being faced by many men in Wales, and likely to be faced by more in the future.

This chapter shows that there has been some redistribution of population from industrial to rural areas, although the small number of people from ethnic minorities remain concentrated in urban areas. The Welsh population is among the least healthy in the UK, despite

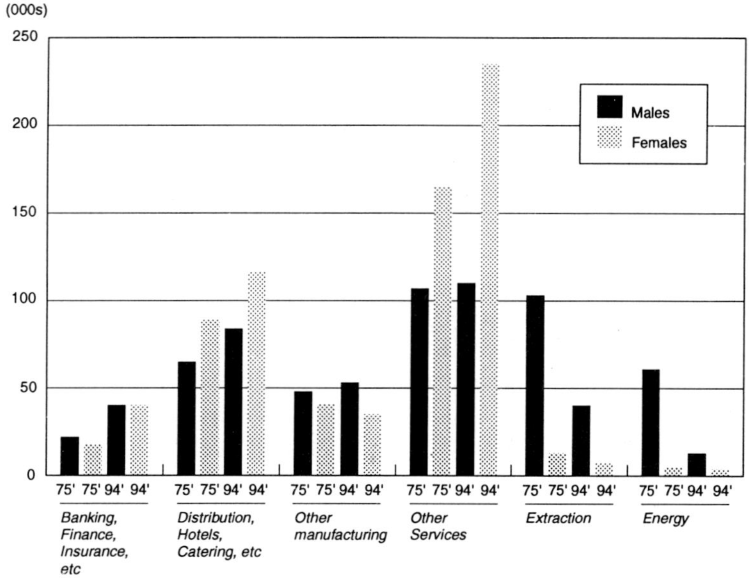

Figure 2.1 Shifts in the Welsh economy: distribution of employees in employment by sex, 1975 and 1994 (000s)
Source: NOMIS: Employee estimates.

the initiatives of Health Promotion Wales. This is reflected in high rates of limiting long-term illness and hence low rates of economic activity for both men and women. These low activity rates contribute to the low gross domestic product of Wales, which is manifested in the number of people having to survive on a subsistence living.

Changes in industrial structure

The tremendous shifts in the Welsh economy from the mid-1970s to the mid-1990s are revealed in Table 2.1. The number of people working in banking, finance and insurance has more than doubled, from 40,000 to 81,000: the biggest sectoral growth in the period. By contrast, huge losses in extraction and manufacture are also shown, especially for men, where the number of jobs declined from 103,000 to 40,000. Heavy losses have been sustained, too, by men in the energy and water supply industries. Employment in manufacturing in Wales is higher than the UK average: it remains a significant part of

Table 2.1: Shifts in the Welsh economy: distribution of employees in employment by sex, 1975–1994

SIC 1980	Females June 1975	June 1994	% Change	Males June 1975	June 1994	% Change	Persons June 1975	June 1994	% Change
Banking, finance, insurance, leasing	18	40	123.4	22	40	84.0	40	81	101.7
Distribution, hotels/ catering; repairs	89	116	30.4	65	84	28.5	154	200	29.6
Other manufacturing industries	41	35	–13.6	48	53	10.5	89	88	–0.6
Other services	165	235	42.3	107	110	3.1	272	345	26.9
Metal goods/ vehicle industries	30	23	–21.8	82	63	–22.9	112	87	–22.6
Agriculture, forestry and fishing	7	3	–52.7	19	14	–24.8	26	18	–32.3
Transport/ communication	9	9	–0.5	52	34	–33.7	61	43	–28.8
Construction	3	5	68.0	58	35	–40.0	61	40	–34.7
Extraction/metal manufacture; minerals/ metals	13	7	–49.1	103	40	–61.3	116	46	–60.0
Energy/ water supply industries	5	4	–28.0	61	13	–78.2	66	17	–74.4

Source: NOMIS: Employee estimates.
Notes: Figures are rounded to the nearest thousand.

Table 2.2: Economic activity rates in the UK: by sex, 1971–1994

	Percentages											
	1971	1979	1981	1984	1986	1988	1989	1990	1991	1992	1993	1994
Females												
Wales	36.7	41.9	42.9	44.1	45.1	44.5	48.2	48.7	48.1	48.5	48.7	48.9
England	44.3	47.5	47.9	49.4	50.0	51.6	53.0	53.3	53.1	53.0	53.3	53.5
Scotland	43.6	49.8	47.4	47.3	47.7	49.3	50.8	51.6	51.2	51.1	51.2	51.4
Northern Ireland	36.8	42.5	43.5	43.8	44.9	44.7	46.0	47.4	47.4	47.5	47.7	48.0
United Kingdom	43.7	47.3	47.5	48.8	49.5	50.8	52.4	52.8	52.5	52.5	52.7	52.9
Males												
Wales	78.4	75.7	73.3	70.6	69.0	68.9	70.1	69.9	69.0	69.0	68.8	68.7
England	80.6	77.5	76.7	74.7	74.2	74.5	74.7	74.7	74.3	74.2	74.1	73.9
Scotland	80.5	78.6	76.9	75.2	73.0	73.1	73.2	73.3	72.6	72.4	72.3	72.1
Northern Ireland	80.7	76.8	76.5	73.8	73.5	72.6	73.2	72.1	71.3	71.0	71.1	71.1
United Kingdom	80.5	77.4	76.5	74.5	73.8	74.0	74.3	74.3	73.8	73.7	73.6	73.4

Sources: Figures from 1971 to 1983[1] are from *Regional Trends* 25, p.149 (1990); originally from the *Labour Force Survey* and Department of Employment.
Figures from 1984 to 1991[2] are from *Regional Trends* 30, p.79 (1995); originally from the *Labour Force Survey*, Employment Department, and the Department of Economic Development, Northern Ireland.
Figures from 1992 to 1994 are projected from 1991 estimates.

Notes: [1]Home population aged 16 or over who are in the civilian labour force. GB Labour Force definitions up to 1984.
[2]ILO definitions from 1984 onwards.

the economy. Meanwhile the growth of jobs in distribution, hotels and catering and in 'other services' (which includes public administration) is clearly significant, and many of these new jobs have been taken up by women. Many industries in both these sectors are characterized by low pay and part-time work.

Economic activity

Patterns of economic activity reflect the changes in industrial sector, with a decline in men in or seeking full-time employment and an increase in women in part-time work. Women in Wales have always had relatively low economic activity rates[2] compared with those of women elsewhere in Britain. This is undoubtedly part of the legacy of an industrial structure dominated by coal which employed few women but made demands upon them to service the needs of the workforce or to contribute in ways that were not revealed in statistics. The nationalization of the coal industry and the installation of pit-head baths and refectories released many women from what has been described as round-the-clock servicing punctuated by catnaps (see John 1984). Although the proportion of women in the workforce has increased in Wales in the last decade, reflecting changed opportunities in the labour market, nevertheless, the rate is still below that for the UK as a whole. This is shown in Table 2.2.

The female economic activity rate increased from 36.7 per cent in 1971, to 42.9 per cent in 1981, to 48.9 per cent in 1994. This gradual rise reflects patterns in the UK more generally but the current figure for Wales has only now reached the 1984 level for the UK. The current UK rate is now just over half, at 52.9 per cent. Only Northern Ireland has a female economic activity rate lower than that of Wales. Male rates of economic activity have always been lower in Wales than elsewhere in the UK, as Table 2.2 shows; however, the gap is wider now than it has been at any time over the last twenty years. Only 68.7 per cent of men were recorded as being economically active in 1994, compared with 78.4 per cent in 1971.

Of course there is a well-known problem with statistics here (see Levitas and Guy 1996; Rees 1992). Much of women's contribution to the economy goes unrecorded. Part-time work below a certain number of hours a week or pay threshold is not recorded.[3] The extent of homeworking is extremely difficult to estimate (see chapter 3;

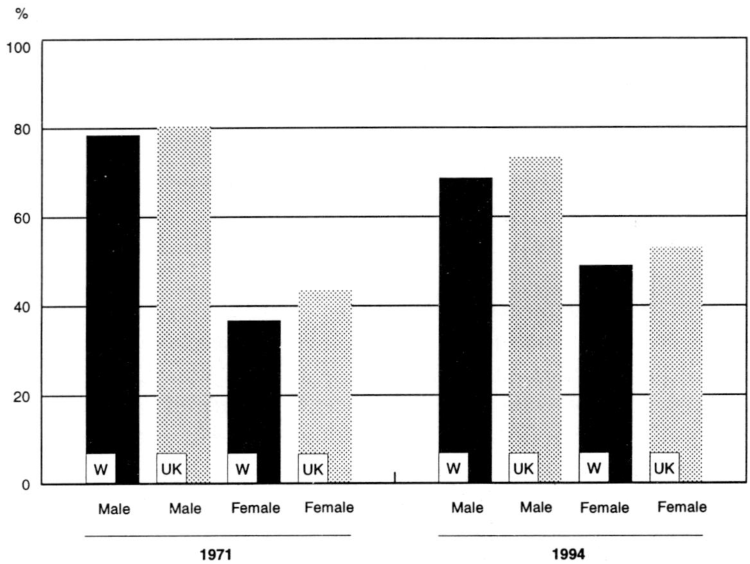

Figure 2.2 Economic activity rates in Wales and the UK by sex, 1971 and 1994
Sources: as Table 2.2.

Felstead 1996a; Phizacklea and Wolkowitz 1995). Much caring work undertaken by women, even if it is paid for, falls below the threshold for insurance and taxation and therefore is unlikely to be revealed in any recorded statistics. Similarly women contribute considerably to family businesses such as farms (see Ashton 1994a on women working on farms in north Wales) or corner shops or to the enterprises of their self-employed partner, but they are not recognized as being employed in their own right. As self-employment is high among men in rural Wales in particular, there is likely to be particularly significant undercounting of women's contribution to the economy in these areas. The European Union has been attempting to regularize this position and extend rights to sickness benefit, a pension and maternity leave to these 'family workers' through legislation.

Hence, in describing female economic activity rates in Wales, our figures on the number of women in paid work or unemployed but wanting work (see below) reported on here, and those presented in following sections of this report, are undoubtedly underestimates.

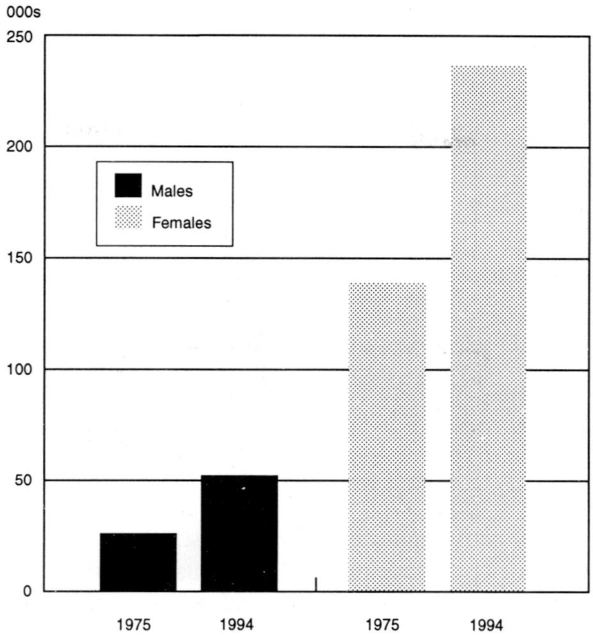

Figure 2.3 Number of employees in employment working part time, 1975 and 1994

Sources: as Table 2.3.

Employment: Full-time and part-time work

The UK specializes in a long-hours culture. We work longer hours, have shorter holidays and retire later than workers in all the other member states of the European Union (Marsh 1991; Rubery et al. 1998). Men in the UK work on average 45.8 hours per week compared with a European Union (EU) norm of 41.3, while women in full-time employment work 40.6 hours on average, as against an EU norm of 39.0. In both cases the UK figures are the longest of all member states (Office for National Statistics 1998: Table 4.17).

We also have less childcare. A review of childcare in EU member states in 1996 reported: 'Most countries have achieved or are moving towards comprehensive publicly-funded services for children aged 3–6 years either in pre-primary schooling or kindergarten: the main exceptions are Ireland, the Netherlands and the UK' (EC Childcare Network 1996: 2). This combination of a long-hours culture and lack

Table 2.3: Trends in part-time working in Wales: employees in employment[1] 1975–1994 (thousands)

	1975	1978	1981	1984	1987	1989	1991	1992	1993	1994
Females										
Number	139	152	159	163	184	209	220	222	229	237
%females	36.7	37.9	40.9	42.6	44.9	44.9	47.1	47.3	48.1	49.6
Males										
Number	26	25	26	29	39	37	43	48	52	52
%males	4.3	4.1	4.8	5.8	7.8	7.1	8.7	10.0	10.7	10.4

Sources: Welsh Office, *Welsh Economic Trends*, No. 4, 1977; No. 12, 1990; No. 15, 1994; No. 16, 1995. Data originally from the Employment Department and the Central Statistical Office.
Note: [1]At June of each year for females and September for males.

of childcare historically explains, in part at least, why the proportion of women who work part-time in the UK is unusually high.

The gradual increase in the proportion of women (and men) who work part time from 1975 to 1994 is shown in Table 2.3. The proportion of female employees working part time increased from 36.7 per cent to 49.6 per cent. In other words, by 1994, almost half the women working in Wales had part-time jobs. The proportion of male employees working part time more than doubled, from 4.3 per cent to over 10 per cent during the two decades. Women in part-time work increased between 1981 and 1991 from 160,000 to 220,000 (calculated from NOMIS: *Census of Employment*). However, the proportion of women in full-time work in Wales fell over the same period by 15,100, to just over a quarter of a million women. The number of women working full time remained remarkably stable during the 1980s in most sectors, for example, manufacturing, distribution, hotels and catering and energy and water supplies. There were, nevertheless, fewer full-time jobs for women in public administration and agriculture, forestry and fishing by 1991 (see Table 2.4).

Most of the growth in part-time employment occurred in distribution, hotels and catering (69.7 per cent increase) and in other service industries (57.3 per cent increase). These were already significant employers of women. In 1991, these two sectors between them employed 81.8 per cent of the women working part time in Wales (compared with 74.9 per cent in 1981).

Table 2.4: Changes in the distribution of females in full-time and part-time employment in Wales, 1981–1991

SIC 1980	Full-time females			Part-time females		
	Sept. 1981	Sept. 1991	% change	Sept. 1981	Sept. 1991	% change
Agriculture, forestry and fishing	3300	2500	–22.9	1200	1200	0.1
Energy and water supply	3800	3300	–14.4	1100	800	–33.0
Manufacturing industries	54000	54800	1.6	10600	10400	–2.1
Construction	2300	2900	28.0	2000	2100	6.5
Distribution, hotels/ catering; repairs	41200	40300	–2.2	53800	76900	43.0
Transport/ communication, banking, finance	23200	34300	47.7	8500	14500	69.7
Public administration and defence	33800	26500	–21.5	15400	10900	–29.5
Other service industries	69700	85500	22.6	65700	103400	57.3

Source: NOMIS: *Census of Employment.*
Note: Figures are rounded to the nearest 100.

Unemployment

Registered unemployment rates for men and women more than doubled in Wales in the twenty years from 1975. However, the rates in the UK as a whole trebled, so that the gap between Wales and the UK has now closed. This is shown in Tables 2.5 and 2.6 which can be used to compare unemployment in 1975 and 1995 in Wales, England, Scotland and Northern Ireland and the UK as a whole.

It has to be remembered that there have been about twenty-seven changes in the rules governing eligibility to unemployment benefit during this period, so that the figures are indicative rather than conclusive. Nevertheless, Table 2.7 indicates that female unemployment in Wales increased from 1.8 per cent in 1975 to a peak of 10.2 per cent in 1986. Since that time there have been a number of fluctuations before settling at the 1995 figure of 4.4 per cent (just below the UK average of 4.5 per cent). Male rates in the same period rose from 5.2 per cent to a 1985/6 high of 16.1 per cent before declining to the 1995 rate of 11.2 per cent: the same rate as the UK.

Table 2.5: Unemployment seasonally adjusted, by sex and country, 1975

	Female	% rate	Male	% rate	Persons	% rate
Wales	7500	1.8	39900	5.2	47400	4.0
Scotland	17500	1.9	66800	4.6	84300	3.6
Northern Ireland	8600	3.9	24900	6.3	33500	5.4
Great Britain	124400	1.3	622300	3.9	746700	2.9
United Kingdom	133000	1.4	647200	4.0	780200	3.0

Source: NOMIS: Unemployment, seasonally adjusted consistent series.
Note: Figures refer to June.

Table 2.6: Unemployment seasonally adjusted, by sex and country, 1995

	Female	% rate	Male	% rate	Persons	% rate
Wales	24300	4.4	83000	11.2	107300	8.3
Scotland	45100	4.1	152900	11.1	198000	7.9
Northern Ireland	19300	6.2	68300	15.5	87600	11.6
Great Britain	530500	4.5	1695500	11.0	222600	8.2
United Kingdom	549800	4.5	1763800	11.2	2313600	8.3

Source: NOMIS: Unemployment, seasonally adjusted consistent series.
Note: Figures refer to June.

In January 1995 there were 25,760 women registered as unemployed in Wales compared with 90,065 men. Rather higher proportions of women were likely to have been without work for short periods of time compared with the UK average and, by the same token, relatively few were long-term unemployed. The same pattern was true for men in Wales, although of course the figures are greater and nearly 5 per cent of unemployed men in the Principality have been out of work for over five years. For some it is clear that the prospect of finding work is small indeed: long-term unemployment among men is recognized as a very serious problem.

Just as some of women's employment is obscured from statistics as described earlier, so it is difficult to get a fix on the nature and extent of women's unemployment. The issue of availability for work, which was deemed to be an essential criterion for eligibility for unemployment benefit, was problematic for women who could not afford childcare unless they had an income. This criterion also applies to

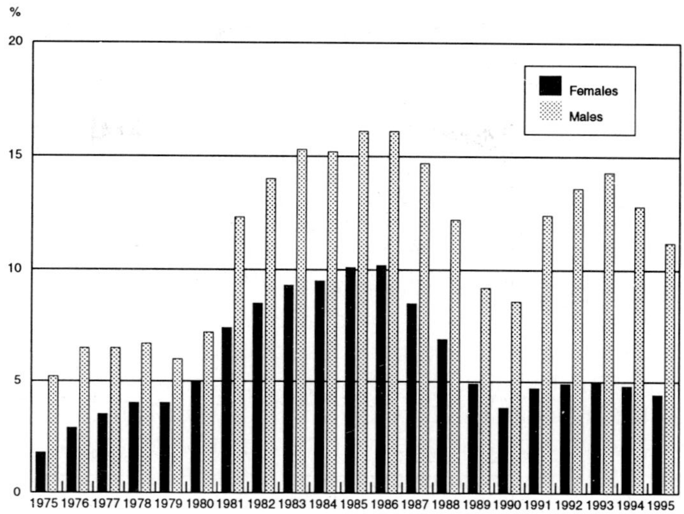

Figure 2.4 Unemployment in Wales, seasonally adjusted, by sex, 1975–1995

Source: NOMIS: Unemployment statistics seasonally adjusted consistent series.

Table 2.7: Unemployment in Wales seasonally adjusted, by sex, 1975–1995

	Female	% rate	Male	% rate	Persons	% rate
1975	7500	1.8	39900	5.2	47400	4.0
1976	12300	2.9	51000	6.5	63300	5.2
1977	15300	3.5	51400	6.5	66700	5.5
1978	17900	4.0	53300	6.7	71200	5.7
1979	18600	4.0	47500	6.0	66100	5.3
1980	23100	5.0	56100	7.2	79200	6.4
1981	33400	7.4	94200	12.3	127600	10.5
1982	37900	8.5	104600	14.0	142500	11.9
1983	42000	9.3	112700	15.3	154700	13.0
1984	44400	9.5	114200	15.2	158600	13.0
1985	47900	10.1	119900	16.1	167800	13.7
1986	49100	10.2	121000	16.1	170100	13.8
1987	42400	8.5	106300	14.7	148700	12.2
1988	35700	6.9	89300	12.2	125000	10.0
1989	26600	4.9	70100	9.2	96700	7.4
1990	20200	3.8	63800	8.6	84000	6.6
1991	25000	4.7	89700	12.4	114700	9.1
1992	26500	4.9	98800	13.6	125300	9.9
1993	27600	5.0	103300	14.3	130900	10.3
1994	26400	4.8	95100	12.8	121500	9.4
1995	24300	4.4	83000	11.2	107300	8.3

Source: NOMIS: Unemployment, seasonally adjusted consistent series.
Note: Figures refer to June of each year.

eligibility for the job-seekers' allowance which replaced unemployment benefit in October 1996. Indeed, despite the importance of part-time work to women, especially in Wales, the job-seekers' allowance reinforces a long-hours culture by insisting that job seekers must be available to work a forty-hour week. Again, many women wanting part-time work are deemed ineligible on this criterion and not only do they not receive the allowance but their status as people looking for work is not recorded in the statistics. This pattern of under-recording is part of the explanation as to why, of all the member states in the EU, the UK is one of only two where male rates of recorded unemployment are higher than those of females.

There is an alternative way of measuring unemployment which is to use the International Labour Office (ILO) definition of being 'without work and seeking a job' (irrespective of eligibility for benefit). This is the definition used in the *Labour Force Survey* (*LFS*). *LFS* data show higher rates of unemployment for women in Wales: 7.5 per cent in 1992 rising to 8.2 per cent in 1994 before falling to 6.5 per cent in 1995 (NOMIS, *Labour Force Survey*). Male rates correspond much more closely to the level indicated by the count of unemployment benefit recipients, suggesting that hidden unemployment is more a characteristic of women than of men.

Demographic change

The population of Wales increased by just over 17,000 between 1971 and 1993 when the population reached 2,906,498 (see Tables 2.8 and 2.9). The 1996 estimate gives a figure of 2,921,100 (Welsh Office 1997: Table 1.2). Most of the increase took place in the 1980s. More significantly, there has been a spatial redistribution of population. While the number of people living in industrial south-east Wales declined, rural parts of Wales such as Powys and Dyfed increased in population. Clwyd's populace has seen the greatest proportionate increase. Women outnumbered men in every county (pre-1996 local government reorganization) throughout this period. In 1993, the gender gap was at its widest in Clwyd (14,151) and Mid Glamorgan (11,927). Women are clearly not a 'minority' group.

Table 2.8: Population by county, 1971–1991

Area	1971 Total persons	1981 Total persons	1981 Females	1981 Males	1991 Total persons	1991 Females	1991 Males	% change per year 1971–1981	% change per year 1981–1991
Clwyd	358601	390200	202800	187400	402927	209860	193067	0.85	0.32
Dyfed	316413	330000	170000	160000	342952	177263	165689	0.42	0.38
Gwent	441385	439700	224700	215000	434244	223592	210652	–0.04	–0.12
Gwynedd	220523	230500	120200	110200	240170	125297	114873	0.44	0.41
Mid Glamorgan	531413	537700	276200	261400	527595	271642	255953	0.12	–0.19
Powys	99178	110500	55600	54900	116801	59147	57654	1.09	0.56
South Glamorgan	390293	384700	199300	185300	388576	202156	186420	–0.15	0.10
West Glamorgan	373398	367300	189600	177700	358600	186022	172578	–0.16	–0.24

Source: 1991 Census Wales, *National Monitor*, OPCS, January 1993, p.12.
Note: All figures relate to areas as constituted at 21 April 1991. All counties have been affected by boundary changes since 1981.

Table 2.9: Mid-year estimates of population by sex and county, 1983–1993

County	Female 1983	Female 1993	Female % change 1983–93	Male 1983	Male 1993	Male % change 1983–93	Persons 1983	Persons 1993	Persons % change 1983–93
Clwyd	205043	215017	4.9	189929	200866	5.8	394972	415883	5.3
Dyfed	172302	180701	4.9	161992	170821	5.5	334294	351522	5.2
Gwent	225193	229636	2.0	214536	220664	2.9	439729	450300	2.4
Gwynedd	120389	124036	3.0	111324	116147	4.3	231713	240183	3.7
Mid Glamorgan	275654	278115	0.9	260188	266188	2.1	536272	544303	1.5
Powys	55535	60429	8.8	55088	59449	7.9	110623	119878	8.4
South Glamorgan	202036	211658	4.8	189316	201565	6.5	391352	413223	5.6
West Glamorgan	190071	190257	0.1	177677	180949	1.8	367748	371206	0.9

Source: NOMIS, Mid Year Population Estimates.
Note: These estimates have been revised to give a series consistent with the figures for both 1981 (based on the 1981 Census) and 1991 (based on the 1991 Census). They relate to areas defined by boundaries as at 1 April 1991.

Welsh-speaking population

Census figures show a slow decline in the numbers of people able to speak Welsh, from 20.9 per cent in 1971, to 18.9 per cent in 1981, to 18.6 per cent in 1991. However, these figures do not reveal the full story. The period also witnessed the setting up of the Welsh-language nursery school movement in 1971 (Mudiad Ysgolion Meithrin), the launch of the Welsh-language television channel Sianel Pedwar Cymru (S4C) in 1982 and, throughout the last twenty years, an extraordinary growth in Welsh-medium primary and secondary schools, especially in largely English-speaking south-east Wales. In 1993, the Welsh Language Act was passed, protecting the rights of Welsh-speakers to be able to conduct their business in Welsh.

No doubt in part as a consequence of the growth in Welsh-medium education, a breakdown of the 1991 Census figures reveals for the first time an increase in the proportion of three- to fifteen-year-olds able to speak Welsh, from 18 per cent in 1981 to 24.9 per cent in 1991. Previously the Welsh-speaking population had been ageing rapidly. Clearly the growth in the numbers of young Welsh-speakers may in time halt the decline of the language. The percentage of pupils in classes where Welsh is the sole or main medium of instruction has grown from 14.1 per cent in 1990/1 to 17.2 per cent in 1995/6. By the same token, the percentage in classes where no Welsh is taught has declined from 22.8 per cent to 7.5 per cent over the same period (Welsh Office 1997: Table 2.74). The impact of the growth in Welsh-medium schools can be seen in the spatial distribution of Welsh-speakers shown in the 1991 Census figures. Although Gwynedd and Dyfed between them account for over half the Welsh-speaking population, the Census shows significant growth in the traditionally Anglicized Cardiff area (see Davies 1995 for an account of the use of the Welsh language in the post-war period and Jones 1993 for a review of the Welsh language in 1992).

The Welsh language is significant to our concerns with the labour market for a number of reasons. It creates jobs, for example in education, commercial services, public administration, personal services, secretarial work, film, broadcasting, the arts and so on. It enhances the market for education and training in Welsh. There will be greater demand for bilingual people in the future as organizations make arrangements to comply with the Welsh Language Act. As later sections show, it is particularly important to ensure that provision of

Table 2.10: Female population by ethnicity and county, 1991 (thousands)

	Entire population	White people	Minority ethnic groups	Black people	Black Caribbean	Black African	Black other	South Asian	Indian	Pakistani	Bangla-deshi	Chinese & others	Chinese	Other Asian	Other other
Dyfed	177.2	176.0	1.2	0.2	0.1	0.0	0.1	0.3	0.2	0.1	0.1	0.7	0.2	0.2	0.3
Gwent	227.3	224.1	3.1	0.6	0.3	0.1	0.2	1.5	0.4	0.8	0.3	1.1	0.3	0.2	0.5
Gwynedd	122.6	121.8	0.9	0.1	0.0	0.0	0.1	0.2	0.1	0.1	0.0	0.5	0.2	0.1	0.2
Mid Glamorgan	275.0	273.0	2.0	0.3	0.1	0.1	0.1	0.7	0.4	0.2	0.1	1.0	0.4	0.3	0.3
South Glamorgan	203.9	194.9	8.9	2.7	0.9	0.8	1.0	3.6	1.4	1.4	0.8	2.6	0.6	0.6	1.4
West Glamorgan	187.3	185.3	2.0	0.3	0.1	0.1	0.1	0.8	0.3	0.1	0.4	0.9	0.3	0.2	0.4
Wales	1465.0	1445.3	19.6	4.5	1.6	1.1	1.8	7.5	3.0	2.7	1.7	7.7	2.3	1.8	3.5

Source: D. Owen (1994), *Ethnic Minority Women and the Labour Market: Analysis of the 1991 Census*, Manchester: EOC.

education and training courses in Welsh are available to meet the current and future needs of consumers and end-users.

Ethnic origin of population[4]

Wales has a small non-white ethnic minority population compared with other parts of the UK: the 1991 Census reveals that 98 per cent of the population of Wales is white and was born in the UK. Betts reports (1994: 25) that Indian and Pakistani Welsh comprise 0.4 per cent of the population and Chinese Welsh a further 0.16 per cent. While there are relatively few members of ethnic minorities in rural Wales, Cardiff's docklands can boast one of the oldest multiracial communities in Britain. The Irish community represent 0.73 per cent of the recorded population and in the south Wales valleys there are strong traditions of in-migration by people of Italian and Ukrainian origin.

Table 2.10, which gives the breakdown of the female population of Wales by ethnicity and county, shows South Glamorgan as being by far the most cosmopolitan of the old counties. Ethnic origin is a significant factor in employment trends. Participation rates vary considerably between different groups as later sections illustrate. It is also important for education and training providers to be aware of potential language training needs in both English and Welsh in particular parts of Wales, and to recognize the resource of language skills among ethnic minorities living in Wales. During the last twenty-five years, a series of Acts related to race relations have been passed (see Landmarks), not all of them helpful to ethnic minorities. The Race Relations Act of 1976 led to the setting up of the Commission for Racial Equality (CRE) and Race Equality Councils were established on a local and regional basis. In 1995 the CRE opened an office in Wales and appointed its first CRE Commissioner for Wales.

Limiting long-term illness and disability

Wales is an unhealthy nation. In all age groups, people of working age from Wales are more likely to report a long-term health problem (or disability: the statistics combine the two) than those from any

Table 2.11: Percentage of the population of working age (16–59/64) who have a long-term health problem or disability, 1995

	All aged 16–59/64	Age groups 16–24	25–34	35–49	50–59/64
Wales	16.0	7.2	8.4	14.1	33.8
England	10.9	5.8	6.0	9.9	22.8
Scotland	11.6	5.1	5.1	9.9	28.0
Great Britain	11.2	5.8	6.0	10.1	23.8

Source: F. Sly, R. Duxley and C. Tillsley (1995), 'Disability and the Labour Market: Findings from the Labour Force Survey', *Labour Market Trends*, p.448 (Table 1).

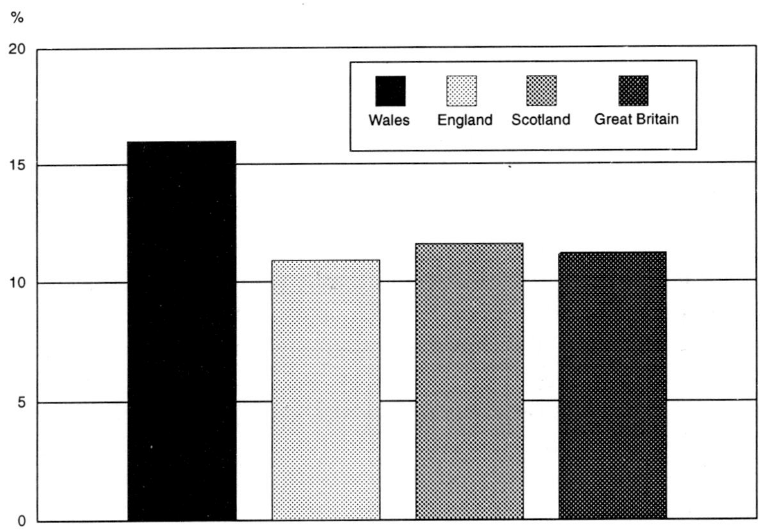

Figure 2.5 Percentage of the population of working age (16–59/64) who have long-term health problem or disability
Source: as Table 2.11.

other part of Britain (see Table 2.11). Rates are especially high among the 35–49 age group (14.1 per cent compared with 10.1 per cent in Britain as a whole) and among the over-fifties (over a third in Wales compared with under a quarter in Britain) (Sly et al. 1995: 448,

Table 2.12: Percentage of females with a limiting long-term illness and ratio of female to male long-term illness rates, by ethnicity and country, 1991

	Entire population	White people	Minority ethnic groups	Black people	Black Caribbean	Black African	Black other	South Asian	Indian	Pakis-tani	Bangla-deshi	Chinese	Chinese & others	Other Asian	Other other
Wales															
% females with a limiting long-term illness	17.4	17.6	7.5	11.2	13.8	10.8	9.1	7.0	7.0	7.8	5.6	5.9	4.0	3.8	8.2
Ratio of female to male long-term illness rate	1.04	1.04	0.81	0.80	0.73	0.82	0.96	0.77	0.81	0.81	0.65	0.89	0.84	0.94	0.92
England															
% females with a limiting long-term illness	13.6	14.0	8.3	9.5	11.5	7.4	5.8	8.5	9.0	7.9	6.9	6.0	4.5	5.7	7.0
Ratio of female to male illness rate	1.14	1.15	0.97	1.00	1.00	1.04	0.91	0.93	1.07	0.82	0.66	1.02	1.02	1.03	1.03
Scotland															
% females with a limiting long-term illness	14.5	14.6	6.6	9.8	15.1	11.6	6.2	7.6	7.9	7.7	3.0	4.5	4.6	3.3	5.0
Ratlo of female to male illness rate	1.12	1.12	0.97	1.13	0.86	1.57	0.87	0.91	1.05	0.86	0.66	1.04	1.12	0.91	1.03
Great Britain															
% females with a limiting long-term illness	13.9	14.2	8.2	9.5	11.5	7.5	5.8	8.4	9.0	7.9	6.9	5.9	4.5	5.6	7.0
Ratio of female to male illness rate	1.13	1.14	0.97	1.00	0.99	1.04	0.91	0.93	1.07	0.82	0.66	1.02	1.02	1.03	1.03

Source: D. Owen (1994), *Ethnic Minority Women and the Labour Market: Analysis of the 1991 Census*, Manchester: EOC (Tables 42 and 43).

original source *Labour Force Survey* 1995). These limiting long-term illness figures are a partial explanation of the relatively low economic activity rates in Wales (see ERES 1994).

According to Health Promotion Wales, in 1996, 28.1 per cent of males and 25.7 per cent of females smoked, and 27.4 per cent of males and 11.2 per cent of females drank more alcohol than the recommended limits (Welsh Office 1997: Tables 2.5 and 2.6). However, poor health is also associated with poverty: the figures on unemployment, and especially long-term unemployment, are of relevance here.

Census data are another source of information on the incidence of limiting long-term illness. While in 1991, in Britain as a whole, 13.9 per cent of women reported such a condition, the figure for women in Wales was 17.4 per cent: this again is higher than that for England or Scotland (1991 Census). Women are more likely to report limiting long-term illness than men in all the constituent parts of Britain, but the gap between women and men is narrower in Wales than elsewhere. The reverse is the case for women from ethnic minority groups in Wales: they are much less likely to report long-term illness than men from the same groups. Rates are slightly higher among the white population than among non-white minority ethnic groups overall (see Table 2.12).

Figures on disability are sparse and the notion of disability is a contested one. Bagihole draws a useful distinction between impairment – the limitation of opportunities due to physical and social barriers – and disability – disadvantage experienced because of social organization which takes no account of impairment and therefore excludes people with them (1997: 42). While there was legislation on equal access for the disabled in 1976 and 1986 (see Landmarks), its effect has been limited. The 1995 Disability Discrimination Act offers more promise and led to the setting up of the National Disability Council and, in 1998, a Disability Rights Commission for Britain as a whole.

Married and solo mothers

Single parenthood has increased substantially over the last twenty years. During that period, in Britain as a whole, economic activity rates for married (and cohabiting) and solo mothers, having started off at a similar position, have diverged. The rate for married mothers has increased while that for single mothers has decreased (Court

Table 2.13: Economic activity of married and lone mothers with dependent children, Spring 1994

	Married mothers					Lone mothers				
	Employed F/T	Employed P/T	Total in employment	ILO Unemployed	Economically inactive	Employed F/T	Employed P/T	Total in employment	ILO Unemployed	Economically inactive
Wales	16.3	35.7	59.5	6.7	33.8	16.4	23.4	42.6	—	49.8
England	18.9	36.0	62.0	4.6	33.4	15.4	20.6	39.3	8.3	52.3
Scotland	21.7	35.2	62.7	5.6	31.7	14.8	21.0	37.5	12.3	50.2
Northern Ireland	24.4	25.7	55.3	–	41.0	–	–	34.1	—	61.0
United Kingdom	19.2	35.6	61.7	4.7	33.5	15.4	20.6	39.1	8.6	52.3

Source: Central Statistical Office (1995), *Regional Trends*, 30, London: HMSO, p.54. Originally, the *Labour Force Survey*, Department of Employment, and Department of Economic Development, Northern Ireland.

Notes: Dependent children are considered those under age 16.
– denotes that sample sizes were too small to provide a reliable estimate.
'Married' includes those cohabiting.
Figures for 'Total in employment' include the self-employed, those on government employment and training programmes, and unpaid family workers.

1995). In Wales in the spring of 1994 a similar picture emerges: 66.2 per cent of married mothers are economically active, compared with 50.2 per cent of solo mothers.

Only 16.3 per cent of married mothers with children of dependent age are in full-time employment in Wales; this is a lower figure than that for England, Scotland or Northern Ireland. Some 35.7 per cent are in part-time work, however, which is broadly comparable to elsewhere. For solo mothers in Wales, the proportion in full-time work is almost identical to that of married mothers, but far fewer (only 23.4 per cent) are in part-time work (see Table 2.13). Single mothers are a major target group in the Labour government's New Deal 'Welfare to Work' programme.

Conclusion

Dramatic changes have taken place in the Welsh economy over the last twenty-five years or so. These have resulted in changes not simply in the balance of sectors but of well-paid and poorly paid jobs, who is in the workforce and what hours are worked. The major significance has been the 'feminizing' of the workforce in that there are now far more women and fewer men in employment than there were. However, both rates are below national averages and this is linked to poor health and the nature of the job opportunities available. Women have moved in effect from the private to the public domain while some men have retreated in the opposite direction. The increase in women working part time is the single most significant change in the nature of the labour force over this period, and many of these women are living in poverty as their wage rates deteriorate, not simply compared with those of men but compared with women working full time. Historically dominated by male-dominated industries such as coal and steel which were characterized by unionization and relatively good wage rates and where workers were recognized for their skills, Wales has taken on the identity of a low-skill/low-wage service-sector-based economy.

Comparisons between men and women can obscure some of the growing disparities among women: the next chapter contrasts men's jobs and women's jobs and looks more closely at the differences among women.

3 Men's work, women's work

Introduction

This chapter focuses on the characteristics of the Welsh workforce and the ways in which it is rigidly divided along gender lines. Despite a few exotic, much-cited exceptions, the vast majority of men and women work in different industrial sectors, have dissimilar kinds of jobs and terms and conditions of employment and receive unequal amounts of pay for the work that they do.

The Welsh workforce

The nature of the working population in Wales has changed considerably over the last twenty years. The workforce is older and made up of fewer men and more women. There are not as many full-time jobs, but more part-time work is available. Unemployment for men and women has more than doubled.

The Welsh workforce is made up of people of working age in employment, the self-employed and those seeking work, known together as the economically active. Chapter 2 showed that economic activity rates in Wales have traditionally been lower than elsewhere in the UK. However, women's participation rate has been increasing to reach the level of the British average, but that of men has been declining to well below the British norm. This is in part a result of the high incidence of people of working age (especially older workers) who have a long-term health problem or disability. Hence we find that younger men and women have higher participation rates than older people, although their rates too have been reduced because of an increased propensity to stay on in education (discussed in chapter 4).

Ethnic origin is a significant determinant of economic activity: the rate for white women is slightly higher than the figure for women in Wales as a whole (65.4 per cent) (using the Census definition), but that for Afro-Caribbean women is higher still. Percentage rates are in the high fifties for Black, Indian and Chinese women (see Table 3.1).

Table 3.1: Percentage of people aged 16–59/64, who are economically active by sex and ethnic origin, Wales and Britain, 1991

	Entire population	White people	Minority ethnic groups	Black people	Black Caribbean	Black African	Black other	South Asian	Indian	Pakis-tani	Bangla-deshi	Chinese & others	Chinese	Other Asian	Other other
Wales															
Female	65.4	65.7	48.2	57.5	67.5	45.6	55.2	40.6	58.5	31.1	16.6	50.3	58.2	40.6	50.3
Male	82.8	82.9	73.7	73.2	81.6	55.5	81.3	71.1	77.9	75.9	77.6	70.6	69.2	68.5	72.8
England															
Female	71.0	72.0	58.0	71.1	75.8	62.2	65.8	48.5	61.3	28.5	22.5	58.6	58.0	57.8	59.9
Male	88.7	89.2	80.5	82.9	87.5	71.3	84.2	80.1	82.9	75.9	74.6	77.8	73.3	79.1	79.6
Scotland															
Female	69.4	69.7	42.8	58.8	68.0	53.1	61.7	36.0	50.6	29.0	27.3	47.7	50.1	38.4	51.7
Male	86.5	86.7	73.7	66.7	79.2	53.3	81.4	79.0	80.7	78.4	74.0	69.0	69.1	62.2	72.6
Great Britain															
Female	70.6	71.4	57.6	70.9	75.7	61.9	65.5	48.1	61.1	28.6	22.4	58.0	57.6	57.0	59.4
Male	88.2	88.7	80.2	82.6	87.5	70.8	84.1	80.1	82.8	76.0	74.7	77.2	72.9	78.5	79.2

Source: Derived from D. Owen (1994), *Ethnic Minority Women and the Labour Market: Tables Derived from the 1991 Census*, Manchester: EOC (Tables 5.1, 5.4, 5.10, 5.14).

Table 3.2: Employment status of men and women in Wales, 1994,[1] (thousands)

	Employees		Self-employed		In employment[2]	
	No.	%	No.	%	No.	%
Male	494	51.2	142	78.5	655	55.6
Female	471	48.8	39	21.5	522	44.4
All	965	100.0	181	100.0	1177	100.0

Source: Calculated from Welsh Office (1995) *Welsh Economic Trends No. 16 1995* Cardiff: Welsh Office, Table 2.6.

Notes: [1]These estimates are derived from a survey and are therefore subject to sampling error.
[2]Includes those who were on government training schemes and unpaid family workers.

For Pakistani and Bangladeshi women, economic activity rates are considerably lower. This pattern of distribution among ethnic groups is similar to that of ethnic minority women in the rest of the UK (see Court 1995; Owen 1994).

In chapter 2 we also established that there are different economic activity rates for married and solo mothers (Table 2.13). About 16 per cent of married and solo mothers with dependent children are in full-time employment; however, 36 per cent of married mothers compared with 23 per cent of solo mothers are in part-time work. Lone parents who work part-time are particularly vulnerable to the poverty trap; loss of benefits and childcare costs are disincentives to working in low-paid occupations.

The distribution of men and women by employment status and occupation for spring 1994 is set out in Table 3.2. This shows that men comprise just over half and women just under half of those in employment. Of employees, the proportions of men and women are very similar: however, this category includes unpaid family workers (most likely to be women) and those on government training schemes. The growth in women's employment has come from part-time rather than full-time work. Self-employment rates for women have remained more or less static over the last two decades while those for men have increased. Men make up nearly 80 per cent of all the self-employed in Wales. The most recent figures suggest that 19.6 per cent of men in employment are self-employed, compared with 7.3 per cent of women (NOMIS Employment Workforce Estimates). Economically active women from minority ethnic groups in Wales are more likely to be self-employed than white women. Self-employment is highest among Chinese, Pakistani and South Asian women in Wales. Black and Black Caribbean women in Wales are more likely to work full time than the Welsh female average.

Gender segregation

The labour force is highly divided by gender both in terms of sector and occupation within sectors. Men and women work in different industries, and in different occupations within those industries. All economies have labour forces segregated by gender although the patterns and degree of rigidity vary, and the gendering of specific occupations can be different in different countries. In Egypt, for example, dentists and engineers tend to be women. The use of gender as a crucial determinant in the allocation of people to sectors and jobs clearly limits the pool from which employers can draw. It is thereby economically inefficient as well as socially unjust (see Humphries and Rubery 1996). Gender is not the only characteristic used to allocate people to positions: age, ethnic origin and disability are also used as discriminators.

There is a further dimension to gender segregation in the labour market. While some jobs are full-time, permanent and offer sick pay and pensions, others are based on part-time hours and/or short-term contracts: these include 'nil-hours' contracts whereby employers make no commitment to offer work in any given week but 'employees' have to make themselves available just in case (Hutton 1995). Short-term, temporary and many part-time contracts tend to involve few opportunities for training or promotion and limited prospects of perks such as paid holidays. While men for the most part have access to the first kind of contract, it is women who form the majority of workers with the second type.

Patterns of gender segregation in Wales, by industrial sector, occupation and type of contract, are particularly marked as the next sections show.

Sectoral differences

The last chapter outlined changes in the broad sectoral differences between men and women over the last twenty-five years. The

Table 3.3: Changes in the sectoral distribution of females in full-time and part-time employment in Wales, 1981–1991

SIC 1980	Full-time females Sept. 1981	Full-time females Sept. 1991	Full-time females % change	Part-time females Sept. 1981	Part-time females Sept. 1991	Part-time females % change
Agriculture, forestry and fishing	3300	2500	–22.9	1200	1200	0.1
Energy and water supply	3800	3300	–14.4	1100	800	–33.0
Manufacturing industries	54000	54800	1.6	10600	10400	–2.1
Construction	2300	2900	28.0	2000	2100	6.5
Distribution, hotels/ catering: repairs	41200	40300	–2.2	53800	76900	43.0
Transport/communication, banking, finance	23200	34300	47.7	8500	14500	69.7
Public administration and defence	33800	26500	–21.5	15400	10900	–29.5
Other service industries	69700	85500	22.6	65700	103400	57.3

Source: NOMIS: *Census of Employment*.
Notes: Figures are rounded to the nearest 100.

decimation of male-dominated sectors and the growth of feminized work were noted. This section focuses in more detail on current patterns within Wales. The domination of the service sector is evident but the significance of manufacturing is also clear. There are spatial variations in the domination of various industries. Powys and Dyfed between them employ over half the Welsh agricultural employees, while over 30 per cent of employees in Mid Glamorgan and Gwent are in manufacturing (OPCS 1994).

Table 3.3 gives a breakdown of employment of women working full time and part time by industrial sector, comparing 1981 with 1991. The substantial growth in 'other services' for both full- and part-time jobs for women is clearly evident. This sector is now by far the biggest employer of women in all counties, in both full- and part-time work, with the one exception of part-time employment in manufacturing in Mid Glamorgan (NOMIS, *Census of Employment 1981, 1991*). It is interesting that the sector 'other services', which is so significant for women's employment, is given such an inadequate description in official statistics. It includes local government and personal services.

The clustering of women in manufacturing and in distribution, hotels, catering and repairs is also noticeable. However, we can clearly observe the substantial growth of part-time work among distribution, hotels, catering and repairs: full-time work for women in this sector has grown only slightly, been stable or even declined in some counties over the same ten-year period. Trends in manufacturing employment for women are also varied. Some counties exhibit growth or stability in this sector, while others record a decline in both full-time and part-time jobs for women (NOMIS, *Census of Employment 1981, 1991*). Nevertheless, manufacturing remains a much more significant employer for both men and women in Wales than elsewhere in the UK. The promise of 6,000 jobs for the Newport area from the Korean inward investment company, Lucky Goldstar, may possibly in time further boost this sector.

Occupational differences

The distribution of men and women between the major occupational groupings for employees and the self-employed in spring 1994 is shown in Table 3.4. Women and men work in different occupational groups. Hence women are clustered into four major categories:

Table 3.4: Occupational segregation in Wales, 1994[1]

	Males		Females	
	No.	%	No.	%
Manager and administrators	117	17.9	52	10.0
Professional occupations	69	10.5	48	9.2
Associate professional and technical	42	6.4	55	10.5
Clerical and secretarial	44	6.7	124	23.8
Craft and related	152	23.2	13	2.5
Personal and protective services	40	6.1	80	15.3
Sales occupations	29	4.4	60	11.5
Plant and machine operatives	100	15.3	27	5.2
Other occupations	58	8.6	62	11.9
All occupations[2]	655	100.0	522	100.0

Source: Calculated from Welsh Office (1995) *Welsh Economic Trends No. 16 1995*, Cardiff: Welsh Office, Table 2.6.

Notes: [1]These estimates are derived from a survey and are therefore subject to sampling error. In cases the sample is too small to allow any reliable estimates to be published. For this reason, and because of rounding, the numbers and percentages do not quite reach the figures shown in the total column.

[2]Includes those who were on government training schemes and unpaid family workers.

clerical and secretarial occupations employ 23.8 per cent of all women in employment; personal and protective services 15.3 per cent; 'other occupations' 11.9 per cent and sales occupations 11.5 per cent. These four groups account for 62.5 per cent of women's employment in Wales. Men by contrast are more likely to be in craft and related skilled work (23.2 per cent), managerial and administrative posts (17.9 per cent) and plant and machine operatives (15.3 per cent). These are for the most part better-paid jobs, which are more likely to offer training and promotion opportunities.

The Hansard Society Commission on Women at the Top published research in 1990 which demonstrated the existence of a 'glass ceiling' facing women seeking promotion in almost every sector. The small percentage of women in top jobs in all walks of life was severely criticized. The figures were difficult to amass, another indication that gender monitoring is not inbuilt in employers' systems of human resource management.[5] Nevertheless,

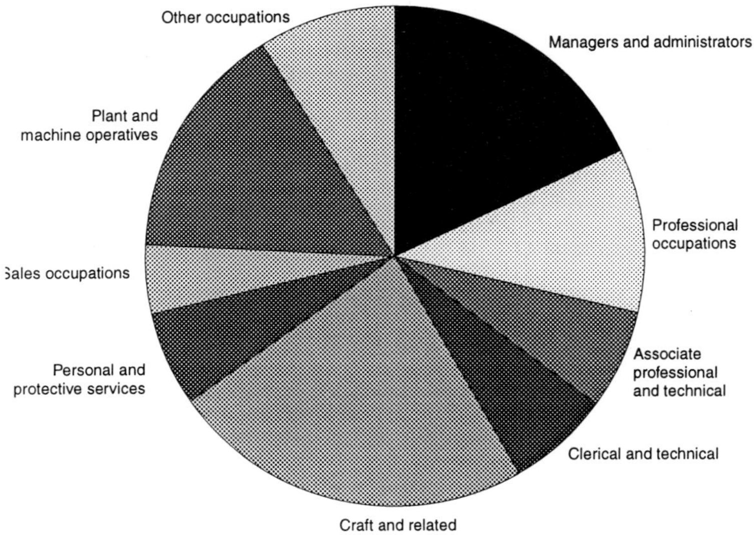

Figure 3.1 Occupational segregation in Wales, 1994 (males)
Source: as Table 3.4.

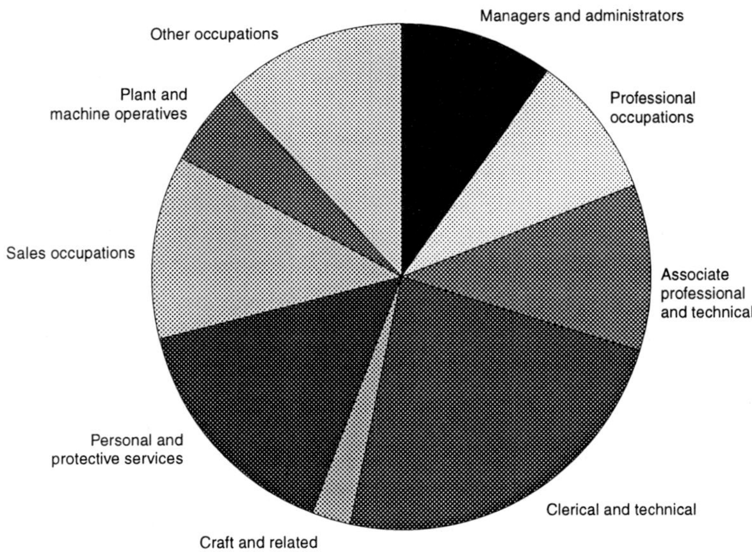

Figure 3.2 Occupational segregation in Wales, 1994 (females)
Source: as Table 3.4.

Table 3.5: Women in top jobs in Wales, 1991

	%
Civil service (Grades 1–4)	3.0
Local government (principal officers)	3.5
Solicitors (partners and single practitioners)	9.6
Management (company directors)	2.3
Higher education (professors)	1.3
Education (secondary school heads)	6.9
Health service (consultants)	13.3

Source: T. Rees and S. Fielder (1991), *Women and Top Jobs in Wales*, report for HTV *Wales This Week*, Cardiff: University of Wales, Cardiff, School for Social and Administrative Studies.

those that were produced told a sorry tale (Hansard Society Commission on Women at the Top 1990).

Occupational categories used in official statistics are fairly broad: it is difficult to acquire data on how many women are successful in getting top jobs or indeed to define what counts as a 'top job'. The Hansard Society Commission's second, updated report (McRae 1996) illustrates some modest progress on women in top jobs in Britain during the 1990s. For example, the percentage of women in grades 1 to 3 in the civil service rose from 10 per cent to 15 per cent between 1988 and 1994; the percentage of women barristers called to the bar increased from 37 per cent in 1987 to 46 per cent in 1995 and the proportion of female executive directors on main boards doubled from 0.5 per cent in 1989 to 1.0 per cent in 1995. There are now one woman chief constable and two women deputy chief constables in the police service (all figures for Britain, from McRae 1996).

Comparable figures for Wales are difficult to obtain.[6] Those that do exist suggest that there are proportionately even fewer women in top jobs in Wales than in the rest of Britain (see Rees 1994a; T. Rees and Fielder 1991; 1992). This is undoubtedly in part a result of the legacy of the industrial structure which so restricted opportunities for women in the labour market. However, given the recent expansion in employment in sectors which employ women in large numbers, that cannot be the only explanation. While structural, cultural and organizational factors play a part, there is clearly a complex set of social processes at work whereby the profile of people in top jobs reproduces itself.[7]

A study conducted in 1991 examined a range of sectors and produced the figures shown in Table 3.5. This shows that the proportion of women in top jobs compared poorly with those for Britain as a whole, as revealed in the Hansard Society Commission report. The study also showed that women tended to fare (marginally) better in the public sector than the private sector. Of course these figures are now out of date. Since then, we do know that the effect of local government reorganization in Wales in 1996 has been to reduce the proportion of women in chief officer posts. However, until the dust settles, it is difficult to chart the position of women following the reorganization of the health service in 1996 and the reconfiguration of health trusts in 1998.

Women in public life

Women's position in the labour market can affect the extent to which they are called upon or feel able to contribute to public life. McRae (1996) reports that the proportion of women among those taking up public appointments in Britain rose from less than 25 per cent in 1991 to about 33 per cent in 1996. By contrast, the proportion of appointments made by the Secretary of State for Wales which went to women rose from 18 per cent in 1990 to 24 per cent in 1996 (Hansard Written Answers, Secretary of State for Wales, 11 June 1996, Col.84) and 26.5 per cent in 1997 (Balsom 1997). A closer look at these appointments reveals that women are particularly poorly represented on tribunals which make important decisions relating to employment, including the adjudication of sex discrimination cases (see Table 3.6). Moreover, only fourteen women from Wales have been given public appointments on UK bodies, compared with seventy-seven men.

In the 1998 edition of the HTV *Wales Yearbook*, the editors, for the first time, provided a gender breakdown of members of public bodies, political institutions and other decision-making organizations. This established baseline data from which it will be possible to monitor the gender balance in public life in the future. The figures for 1997 for public bodies are summarized in Table 3.7. It shows that of the twenty-one chairs of Welsh bodies and Welsh commissioners for British bodies, eighteen (86 per cent) are male. Some 90 per cent of the chief executives are male (one post is vacant), as are three-quarters of the members of the boards of these Welsh-based decision-making bodies.

Table 3.6: Public appointments made by the Secretary of State for Wales, 1 September 1997

Type of body	Male	Female	Total	% female	% female at 1 June 1996
Welsh executive	117	44	161	27.3	23.2
Welsh advisory	65	21	86	24.4	26.7
Welsh health	142	56	198	28.3	30.6
Welsh tribunal	23	5	28	17.9	20.0
Welsh other	93	46	139	33.1	13.2
UK bodies	77	14	91	15.4	20.6
Total	517	186	703	26.5	23.6

Sources: 1996 figures calculated from Welsh Office (1996), *Appointments by the Secretary of State for Wales*, Cardiff: Welsh Office (p.11, Summary of appointments by gender at 1 June 1996).
1997 figures from Balsom (1997: 193).

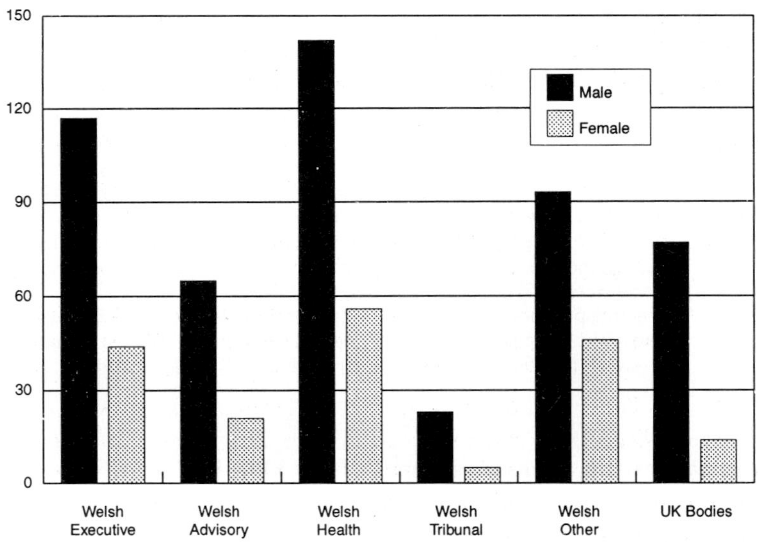

Figure 3.3 Public appointments made by the Secretary of State for Wales, 1 September 1997
Source: as Table 3.6.

Table 3.7: Membership of public bodies in Wales, by sex, 1997

	Chair		Chief Executive		Board members	
	Male	Female	Male	Female	Male	Female
Arts Council of Wales	1		1		12	6
BBC Cymru Wales	1		1		8	4
Cardiff Bay Development Corporation	1		1		9	0
Commission for Racial Equality[1]	1			1	0	0
Countryside Council for Wales	1		1		9	3
Development Board for Rural Wales	1		1		11	2
Equal Opportunities Commission Wales[1]		1		1	0	0
Further Education Funding Council	1		1		7	1
Health Promotion Authority for Wales	1		1		4	0
Higher Education Funding Council	1		1		6	1
Independent Television Commission[2]		1			0	0
Land Authority for Wales	1		1		8	0
National Lottery Charities Board	1		1		2	1
Qualifications, Curriculum and Assessment Authority	1		1		8	5
S4C[3]	1		1		2	3
Sports Council for Wales	1		1		10	5
Tai Cymru	1		1		4	3
Wales Tourist Board	1		1		6	1
Welsh Consumer Council		1	1		9	4
Welsh Development Agency	1		1		8	2
Welsh Language Board	1		1		9	3
Total	18	3	18	2	132	44
% M or F	85.7	14.3	90.0	10.0	75.0	25.0

Source: Calculated from D. Balsom (1997) *The Wales Yearbook 1998,* Cardiff: HTV.

Notes: [1]The EOC is a GB organization with a Commissioner for Wales and Director of the EOC office in Wales. Similarly, the Commission for Racial Equality (not listed in the *Yearbook*) has a Commissioner for Wales and an executive running the office in Wales;
[2]The Independent Television Commission has a National Officer based in Wales (to be appointed) and a National UK Commission Member (female);
[3]A woman has just been appointed as Chair of S4C (spring 1998).

In politics, it is a similar picture. Of forty MPs, four are women; of five MEPs, two are women; of fifty-nine peers described as having 'Welsh connections', two are women (Balsom 1997). There have been no women ministers at the Welsh Office since it was set up in 1970, although there is now a woman permanent secretary.

In local government, three of the twenty-two new unitary authorities have women leaders (or mayors) and three have women chief executives. Of 1,270 members, one in five is a woman (see Table 3.8). The proportions range from 39 per cent in Torfaen and 36 per cent in

Table 3.8: Members of the unitary authorities in Wales, by sex, 1997

	Male	Female	Total	% Female
Blaenau Gwent	39	3	42	7.1
Bridgend	36	12	48	25.0
Caerphilly	55	13	68	19.1
Cardiff	43	24	67	35.8
Carmarthenshire	73	7	80	8.8
Ceredigion	42	2	44	4.5
Conwy	46	14	60	23.3
Denbighshire	37	10	47	12.3
Flintshire	58	14	72	19.4
Gwynedd	72	10	82	12.2
Merthyr Tydfil	26	7	33	21.2
Monmouthshire	30	12	42	28.6
Neath–Port Talbot	53	11	64	17.2
Newport	43	4	47	8.5
Pembrokeshire	54	6	60	10.0
Powys	64	19	83	22.9
Rhondda Cynon Taff	55	20	75	26.7
Swansea	57	16	73	22.0
Torfaen	27	17	44	38.6
Vale of Glamorgan	37	10	47	21.3
Wrexham	36	16	52	30.8
Ynys Môn	38	2	40	5.0
Total	1021	249	1270	19.6

Source: Calculated from D. Balsom (1997), *The Wales Yearbook 1998*, Cardiff: HTV.

Cardiff to 4.5 per cent in Ceredigion and 5 per cent in Ynys Môn. This is not an urban/rural issue, however: urban authorities such as Newport have a low percentage of women councillors (9 per cent) while sparsely populated Powys has 23 per cent.

What is being done about these low proportions of women in public life? The Welsh Office has been seeking to increase the proportion of women on the public appointments register (which is consulted when appointments are made) with some success: there were 1,068 women on the list in 1996 compared with 470 in 1993 (Hansard Written Answers, Secretary of State for Wales, 11 June 1996, Col.84). Following the Nolan report on public life which recommended transparency in public appointments procedures, the last Conservative secretary of state for Wales (Mr William Hague) set up a panel of independent people to advise and take part in the appointments process. This panel was further developed by the Labour secretary of state for Wales, Mr Ron Davies, following the

May 1997 general election, to make the procedure more open to public scrutiny.

At the time of writing (spring 1998), there is considerable debate about ensuring a gender balance in the National Assembly of Wales. However, the legality of various mechanisms such as 'twinning constituencies' is unclear. While a variety of opinions have been expressed, the EOC's guidelines on the matter indicate that it would take a test case to go through the courts to establish the position. What is clear is that traditional procedures are likely to produce a similar pattern to the one described here for other arenas of public life.

Contract segregation: full- and part-time work

The third kind of gender segregation in the labour market is by type of contract. Full-time workers are more likely to enjoy benefits such as paid holidays, sick pay, maternity leave and pensions as well as opportunities for promotion and training. Part-time workers had their entitlements extended as a result of legislation in the UK in 1996 to comply with a European Directive: before that their access to these benefits was entirely at the discretion of the employer. There are clear sectoral differences in practices as to contracts for employees and women predominate in those sectors, such as catering and distribution, which operate on part-time, temporary contracts. Is this cause or effect?

Beechey and Perkins (1987) explored this question in their study in England which compared the contracts of male bakery workers, who had full-time jobs with opportunities for overtime, with the part-time contracts of cake-makers, largely women without any employment benefits, who worked for the same company. It was clear that expectations about the role of work in men's and women's lives was reflected in employers' policies and practices with regard to work organization and reward. Such expectations are based on a notion of a 'traditional' family with breadwinner and home-maker roles. This model describes a small and shrinking number of households and yet is widely used to inform employment practices to the benefit of men, who are deemed to be breadwinners, and to the detriment of women, who are regarded as earning supplementary wages.

Walker's study of women in the Aberystwyth hotel trade shows how closely gender and skill are linked in this sector, and as a consequence, in their type of contract and pay:

> Closely related to the issue of skill is pay: hotel owners were willing to pay higher wages for those employees whose labour was defined as more skilled and more pivotal to the efficient running of the hotel. These 'core' employees often received a higher wage at the expense of the less skilled and more replaceable general body of employees. In other words, hotel owners were willing to invest money in the former group by saving money (through paying low wages) through the latter group . . . the high wages of the 'core', mostly male, group were dependent upon the low wages of the main group of employees, who were mostly women.
>
> (Walker 1992: 149)

It is important to recognize the diversity of work contract arrangements within feminized service sector companies, however. Rees and Fielder (1992) report how different branches of the service sector appear to be moving in contrasted directions with respect to contracts. They conducted case studies of two growing companies which undertook functions which have been contracted out by many major employers: a contract cleaning company and a catering company. The authors found that while women were the vast majority of those employed in operative grades in both companies, in one there was a strategy of work intensification, leading to high staff turnover (267 per cent in one year), while the other moved towards improving employment conditions by enhanced training and promotion possibilities, creating opportunities for 'careers' (G. Rees and Fielder 1992).

The growth in the service sector in Wales has been the major source of new part-time jobs taken by women. However, many of the low-paid jobs are found in this sector, as the next section demonstrates.

Pay segregation

Before the Equal Pay Act came into force in 1975, it was perfectly legal to pay men and women different rates for the same job, and many employers did so. While the legislation certainly contributed towards the narrowing of the pay gap, it did not close it, largely because men and women tend to work in different sectors and occupations. It thus proved difficult for a woman who wanted to bring a case for equal pay to find a man doing exactly the same work with which to compare herself. This led to Equal Pay for Work of

Equal Value amendment regulations in 1983 which enabled comparisons to be made between workers with similar sets of responsibilities. This again, through the development of case law, led to a further narrowing of the pay gap, but in 1995 there was still a 25 per cent difference between the wages of men and women working full time (*ONS New Earnings Survey* 1995).

This is partly due to the contract segregation described earlier. Pay rates in part-time jobs in the service sector in particular have remained depressed over the decades, although women's wages can be low in manufacturing plants too. Indeed low wages, and more particularly low wage costs, are seen as a major incentive to inward investors to open up plants in Wales. However, women in white-collar professional jobs in Wales earn considerably less than their male counterparts too, especially in the private sector.

There are tremendous difficulties in making comparisons of pay rates between men and women. Many women working part time have incomes which fall below the threshold for which statistics are recorded. Homeworkers too (discussed below) often have 'self-employed' status and their incomes are not recorded. They are likely to be among the worst paid, so published figures offer a slightly rosier picture than that which really pertains. Figures on part-time wage rates are highly problematic: for this reason this section focuses on full-time workers while recognizing that part-timers tend to be paid considerably less. However, it is also difficult to make comparisons between full-time workers given different customs and practices in rewarding performance, bonuses, overtime payments and so on. The figures that follow therefore have to be interpreted with some caution. Finally, with reference to the statistics, it is worth noting that published figures are rarely presented in such a way that male/female comparisons can easily be made. The pay gap is thus obscured to all but those who are sufficiently motivated to work out the calculations for themselves.

In Wales, men's rates of pay have gradually declined compared with rates in Britain as a whole, reflecting the patterns of industrial restructuring described in chapter 2. While males in 1975 earned 97.0 per cent of the wages of the GB male average, by 1994 this had declined to 88.6 per cent. When we compare male and female rates of pay in Wales over the last two decades and note the narrowing of the gap, we need to bear this in mind. Female rates compared with those in the rest of GB have also declined but not quite as

Table 3.9: Average gross weekly earnings of full-time males and females for Wales, 1975–1994

	1975		1980		1985		1990		1994	
	£ per week	% of GB	£ per week	% of GB	£ per week	% of GB	£ per week	% of GB	£ per week	% of GB
Manual females	31.3	97.5	67.7	99.6	99.7	98.4	143.5	97.0	175.7	96.6
Non-manual females	37.8	95.6	78.5	94.9	125.3	93.6	193.0	89.6	257.4	92.5
All females	35.8	95.8	75.4	95.7	118.8	94.0	180.3	89.5	239.0	91.4
Manual males	55.9	100.4	111.3	99.6	159.6	97.6	224.7	94.7	272.3	97.0
Non-manual males	64.5	94.4	132.5	93.8	206.7	91.9	306.2	86.3	375.6	87.7
All males	59.0	97.0	119.1	95.7	179.1	93.1	258.6	87.5	320.9	88.6

Sources: Welsh Office, *Welsh Economic Trends, No. 4*, 1977, p.29; *Welsh Economic Trends, No. 8*, 1982/83, p.36; *Welsh Economic Trends, No. 12*, 1990, p.35; *Welsh Economic Trends, No. 13*, 1992, p.30; *Welsh Economic Trends, No. 16*, 1995, p.33. Originally, data is from the *New Earnings Survey*.

Notes: Figures relates to employees whose pay for the survey pay period was not affected by absence. Men aged 21 and over and women aged 18 and over on 1 January of the year of each survey.

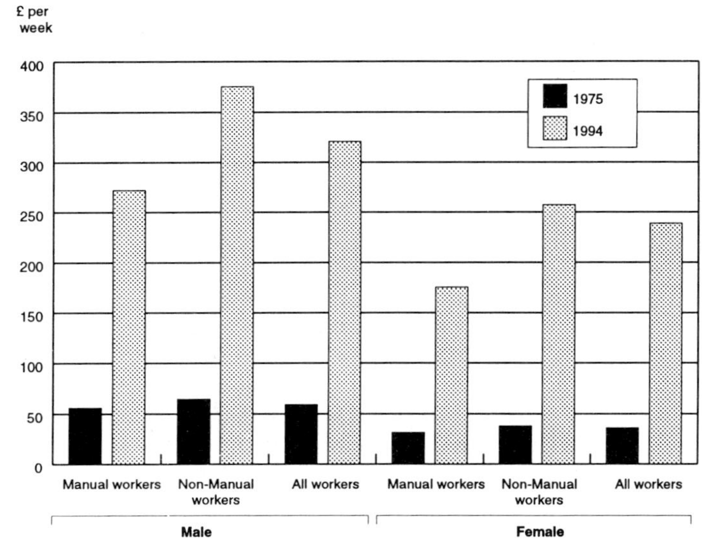

Figure 3.4 Average gross weekly earnings of full-time males and females for Wales, 1975 and 1994
Source: as Table 3.9.

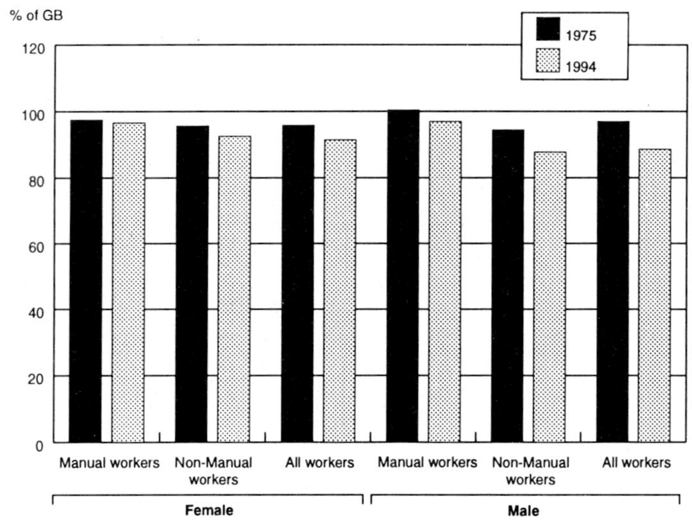

Figure 3.5 Average gross weekly earnings of full-time males and females for Wales, 1975 and 1994: percentage of GB
Source: as Table 3.9.

Table 3.10: Average gross weekly earnings of full-time adults, by statistical subdivision, April 1994

	Manual			Non-manual			All		
	Females	Males	Females as % of males	Females	Males	Females as % of males	Females	Males	Females as % of males
Clwyd	179.2	288.2	62.2	251.6	395.9	63.4	230.7	331.0	69.7
Gwynedd	–	276.4	–	–	–	–	234.7	315.3	74.4
Powys	–	245.8	–	–	–	–	–	288.1	–
West Wales	–	243.4	–	–	360.8	–	229.4	304.0	75.5
Gwent	182.9	270.7	67.6	242.1	365.6	66.2	222.7	307.8	72.3
Mid Glamorgan	175.2	248.7	70.4	267.9	375.7	71.3	244.1	308.3	79.1
South Glamorgan	188.7	276.3	68.3	264.5	377.8	70.0	255.8	339.6	75.3
West South Wales	163.3	288.5	56.7	257.1	381.9	67.3	239.4	330.2	72.5
Industrial South Wales	175.1	271.8	64.4	259.7	375.9	69.1	242.4	322.7	75.1
Wales	175.7	272.3	64.5	257.4	375.6	68.5	239.0	320.9	74.4
Great Britain	181.9	280.7	64.8	278.4	428.2	65.0	261.5	362.1	72.2

Source: Welsh Office, *Welsh Economic Trends, No. 16*, 1995, pp.38–9. Originally, *New Earnings Survey* and Welsh Office.

Notes: Figures refer to full-time employees whose pay for the surveys was not affected by absence. Results are based on the standard industrial classification.

Figures are not shown for subdivisions of under 50 people in the sample or for which the estimate has a standard error of more than 5.0 per cent.

dramatically: in 1975 women earned 95.8 per cent of the GB female average, by 1994, this had slipped to 91.4 per cent (see Table 3.9).

There are manual/non-manual differences in comparative wage rates. Table 3.9 shows how, while men and women in both manual and non-manual jobs earned less than GB averages through the two decades, the one exception was manual male workers in 1975. This was a period when coal and steel were still dominant: one of the effects of job losses from these industries has been the decline in male manual wages in Wales. Non-manual male wage rates have declined proportionate to the British male average even more: from 94.4 per cent in 1975 to 87.7 per cent in 1995. For women manual and non-manual full-time workers there is also a story of decline in wages relative to the British average over the two decades, with just a slight improvement in the 1990s. However, while the gap between manual and non-manual female workers relative to GB averages are not as great as those of men, again manual workers score a little better proportionately.

The low rates of male workers' pay relative to British averages needs to be borne in mind when we compare male and female pay rates within Wales in 1994 (see Table 3.10). Women's wages in Wales for full-time workers represent about 75 per cent of male wage rates, but these male rates are well below the GB averages. There are spatial differences, as the same table shows. Female manual weekly wage rates are particularly low in south-west Wales (£163) as are non-manual rates in Gwent and Clwyd. The average male manual rate in Powys, at £245 gross a week, is among the lowest in Britain.

Low wages in Wales are of considerable concern to the Wales Trades Union Congress (Wales TUC 1994) and the Low Pay Unit (Edwards 1996). The National Local Government Forum Against Poverty (1996) conducted an analysis using a wide range of poverty indicators to conclude that Merthyr Tydfil had the highest poverty score, followed by Blaenau Gwent, Newport and Cardiff.

Homeworkers

It is extremely difficult to calculate the number of homeworkers in Britain; however, there is a general consensus that the vast majority of homeworkers are women (Phizacklea and Wolkowitz 1995). Felstead (1996a) argues that there has been a renewal of interest in and concern about the conditions of homeworkers: for example, the Homeworkers' Bill 1991 sought to grant homeworkers the same rights and duties as other workers. However, debates about a minimum wage tend to assume a focus on employees; there is a concern that homeworkers may be excluded because they are usually regarded as self-employed.

In Britain as a whole, it has been estimated that some 82 per cent of homeworkers are women. They are more likely to have children and less likely to have any qualifications than the female workforce more generally (Felstead 1996a: original source *ONS Labour Force Survey*, Spring 1994). Wales has slightly more than its demographic fair share of homeworkers: Welsh men account for 8.1 per cent of the male homeworkers in Britain while Welsh women constitute 5.1 per cent of Britain's female homeworkers. These figures compare with men in Wales comprising only 4.7 per cent of the male workforce and Welsh women only 4.6 per cent of the female workforce overall (all figures Felstead 1996a). It is clear that homeworkers are at serious risk of exploitation, of health and safety dangers, and that they lack the employment protection extended to employees. The fact that there are a significant number of homeworkers in Wales means that their situation should be a cause for concern. It is doubtful whether the equality legislation has made much impact on the lives of homeworkers (Felstead 1996a; Phizacklea and Wolkowitz 1995).

Unemployment

The economically active population includes the employed, the self-employed and the unemployed. Patterns of unemployment over the last two decades in Wales were described in the last chapter: essentially rates of registered unemployment rose during the mid-1980s for men and women but in 1995 reached UK average rates of 4.4 per cent for women and 11.2 per cent for men (see Table 2.6). 1996 figures for Wales are 4.2 per cent and 11.3 per cent respectively – both slightly higher than UK figures (Welsh Office 1997: Table 4.7).

Unemployment rates vary by county and by ethnic origin within Wales. While figures from the *Labour Force Survey* (using the ILO definition of unemployment of actively seeking work rather than eligibility for benefit) are too small to disaggregate by sex, Table 3.11 indicates that in November 1995 Gwynedd emerges as the county with

Table 3.11: ILO unemployment rates for all persons of working age, by county, 1992–1995

	Sept.–Nov. 1992		Sept.–Nov. 1993		Sept.–Nov. 1994		Sept.–Nov. 1995	
	Persons	% rate	Persons	% rate	Persons	% rate	Persons	% rate
Clywd	16000	8.6	19000	10.1	15000	7.9	14000	7.9
Dyfed	–	–	17000	11.4	15000	9.8	15000	10.0
Gwent	26000	12.6	19000	9.5	18000	8.7	11000	5.4
Gwynedd	10000	10.5	11000	10.8	12000	10.7	15000	15.0
Mid Glamorgan	29000	13.3	27000	11.4	26000	11.2	21000	8.7
Powys	–	–	–	–	–	–	–	–
South Glamorgan	18000	9.3	17000	8.8	21000	10.8	14000	7.2
West Glamorgan	18000	12.1	16000	10.5	18000	12.6	14000	9.9

Source: NOMIS: *Labour Force Survey*.

Notes: These figures are subject to sampling variability. Numbers are rounded to the nearest thousand and percentages to the one decimal place.

– Indicates that the sample size was too small for reliable estimate. (Figures are too small for reliable estimate to disaggregate by sex at county level.)

Table 3.12: Female unemployment rates and ratio of female to male unemployment rates by ethnicity and region, 1991

	Entire population	White people	Minority ethnic groups	Black people	Black Caribbean	Black African	Black other	South Asian	Indian	Pakis-tani	Bangla-deshi	Chinese & others	Chinese	Other Asian	Other other
Wales															
Female unemployment rate %	6.7	6.6	13.1	15.0	11.5	21.2	16.0	14.2	10.2	20.8	24.0	11.1	7.9	11.7	14.2
Ratio of female to male unemployment rate	0.53	0.53	0.73	0.52	0.42	0.66	0.57	0.96	1.17	0.95	1.45	0.73	0.92	1.39	0.6
England															
Female unemployment rate %	6.7	6.2	15.6	16.6	13.5	24.8	18.5	16.5	12.7	30.1	34.9	12.2	8.3	12.3	14.7
Ratio of female to male unemployment rate	0.61	0.59	0.76	0.66	0.57	0.85	0.72	0.85	0.94	1.03	1.11	0.78	0.78	0.85	0.75
Scotland															
Female unemployment rate %	7.6	7.6	14.2	14.1	12.3	16.4	12.5	17.9	13.0	22.4	15.1	10.6	7.3	10.4	15.8
Ratio of female to male unemployment rate	0.61	0.61	0.97	0.87	0.70	1.15	0.72	1.12	1.13	1.20	1.01	0.87	0.86	1.04	0.89
Great Britain															
Female unemployment rate %	6.8	6.3	15.6	16.6	13.5	24.7	18.3	16.5	12.7	29.6	34.5	12.1	8.3	12.3	14.8
Ratio of female to male unemployment rate	0.61	0.59	0.77	0.66	0.57	0.85	0.72	0.86	0.95	1.04	1.12	0.78	0.79	0.86	0.75

Source: Calculated from D. Owen (1994), *Ethnic Minority Women and the Labour Market: Analysis of the 1991 Census*, Manchester: EOC (Tables 8.1, 8.3, 8.9 and 8.11).

Table 3.13: Unemployed claimants by duration and sex, January 1995

	2 weeks or less	Over 2 and up to 8 weeks	Over 8 and up to 13 weeks	Over 13 and up to 26 weeks	Over 26 weeks and up to 1 year	Over 1 and up to 2 years	Over 2 and up to 3 years	Over 3 and up to 5 years	Over 5 years	Total (= 100%) (numbers)
Females										
Wales	9.5	15.3	11.0	21.3	19.1	12.3	4.5	4.5	2.5	25760
England	8.8	13.5	10.1	19.9	20.2	14.0	5.4	5.3	2.7	489421
Scotland	8.9	16.4	12.5	19.1	19.6	11.7	3.9	4.3	3.6	50392
Northern Ireland	6.0	10.4	7.3	17.5	17.9	14.7	7.7	7.4	11.1	19559
United Kingdom	8.7	13.7	10.3	19.8	20.0	13.8	5.3	5.2	3.1	585132
Males										
Wales	5.6	13.5	9.6	17.1	17.1	15.6	7.3	9.8	4.7	90065
England	5.7	12.0	8.7	16.1	17.9	16.2	8.2	10.4	4.7	1582492
Scotland	5.4	14.1	9.7	16.5	18.4	15.2	6.6	8.1	6.1	173340
Northern Ireland	3.3	7.2	5.3	10.6	12.9	15.3	10.1	12.9	22.3	72324
United Kingdom	5.6	12.1	8.7	15.9	17.8	16.1	8.1	10.3	5.5	1918221

Source: Central Statistical Office (1995), *Regional Trends 30*, London: HMSO, p.86; originally, the Employment Department.
Note: Figures are not seasonally adjusted and all but the final column show percentages.

the highest rate of ILO unemployment (15.0 per cent), taking over Mid Glamorgan's traditional lead position. The rate is also high in West Glamorgan (9.9 per cent). The highest *numbers* of unemployed were in Mid Glamorgan (21,000) and in Dyfed and Gwynedd (15,000 each). This indicates that unemployment is both an urban and a rural phenomenon in Wales. The table also shows the general downward trend of unemployment during the 1990s using the ILO definition. Analysis of the 1991 Census shows how women from ethnic minorities report that they suffer much higher rates of unemployment than white women in Wales (Table 3.12). Rates are particularly high among Bangladeshi (24.0 per cent) and Pakistani women (20.8 per cent).

There are gender differences in the duration of registered unemployment, as Table 3.13 shows. While women are more likely to have been unemployed for less than a year in Wales, men feature more heavily among those who have been without work for over a year. Long-term unemployment among men is shown starkly in the table: in 1995 nearly 22 per cent of unemployed men had been without a job for two years or more (compared with only 11.5 per cent of unemployed women).

New initiatives for equal opportunities in employment

There have been a number of initiatives to foster equal opportunities in employment and in particular employment of women in Wales.

The headquarters of the EOC in Britain is based in Manchester and it set up an office in Wales in 1978, the staff of which have been active in developing partnerships to foster equal opportunities in Wales. This includes setting up Chwarae Teg (see below). The Equality Exchange is a network of employers set up and facilitated by the EOC to meet and learn of good practice from each other in working towards equality for men and women in employment. In Wales there are sixty members altogether, including employers of different sizes and sectors from all over Wales. The EOC in Wales also works actively with the Confederation of British Industry in Wales, the Wales Trades Union Congress, individual trade unions, the small-business sector and further education colleges on equal opportunities. Following the Welsh Language Act in 1993, the EOC produced guidelines for employers on how to advertise jobs in the Welsh language in a gender-neutral way (Awbery 1997). Cases brought by individuals based on the sex discrimination and equal pay legislation have been supported (see EOC 1997a).

Chwarae Teg (Welsh for 'fair play') is a consortium of organizations from the public and private sector working together to expand the role of women in the workforce. It focuses on some of the major barriers to women's participation in work – training and childcare (see Chwarae Teg 1997a). The founding partners that set up Chwarae Teg in 1992 included the EOC in Wales, the Welsh Development Agency and Business in the Community. It is now supported with funding from Welsh Office as well as a wide range of consortia members including local authorities, training and enterprise councils, public and private sector employers and voluntary organizations. It has met with such success that the English regions and now Scotland and Northern Ireland have their own versions and it has been identified by the European Commission as a model of good practice in partnership working. Belgium and the Netherlands are now setting up fair play initiatives.

Opportunity 2000 was launched in Wales in May 1992 by Business in the Community backed by the government, with the aim of increasing the quantity and quality of women's participation in the workforce. Some employers who sign up to Opportunity 2000 develop and implement policies to help them meet targets to improve the number of women in management by the end of the century. The annual reports of Opportunity 2000 show that progress for some of the signatories has been somewhat impeded by major retrenchments in their industries. In Wales the Opportunity 2000 initiative is supported by Business in the Community, often through secondment of personnel from member companies.

MEWN Cymru is a network of Black and ethnic minority women in Wales facilitated by a member of staff based at the EOC and supported by the Commission for Racial Equality. Following an initial conference held in 1993 (EOC 1993), the network seeks to ensure that the voices of women from ethnic minorities in Wales are heard, particularly by those responsible for the delivery of public services (Baruah 1997).

At the United Nations Fourth World Conference on Women held in 1995 in Beijing, a Global Platform for Action was agreed upon, and the delegates, from non-governmental organizations throughout the world, are seeking to ensure that this is now implemented in their respective countries. The National Agenda for Action for the UK was drawn up by the Women's National Commission and the Equal

Opportunities Commissions for Great Britain and Northern Ireland in consultation with a wide range of women's organizations. In Wales, a programme complementing the National Agenda was developed by a partnership of women's organizations: the Wales Assembly of Women, the EOC, the National Federation of Women's Institutes Wales, Welsh Women's Aid, Chwarae Teg, MEWN Cymru, Merched y Wawr and Wales Women's Euro Network (see Wales Assembly of Women et al. 1996). This was the first time that all these organizations, representing very different constituencies, had worked together. The programme is made up of ten policy papers concentrating on the legal framework; women's participation in decision-making; childcare, family and caring; education and training; media; violence against women; health; poverty, pay and non-traditional work; double disadvantage and monitoring and mainstreaming. The programme identifies priorities within this framework for tackling the major sources of gender discrimination and disadvantage in Wales.

Women have been very much a minority presence in the various business clubs in Wales where important contacts can be made, despite the increase in the number of women running their own companies. A recent development has been the mushrooming of women's business networks, such as the Cardiff-based Women in Enterprise and the thriving Gwent Women's Enterprise Network which attracts about 100 members to its annual dinners. The membership consists of women running their own businesses or in senior positions in business and the professions. These networks have partly evolved in response to the exclusion of women from the senior ranks of the business community in Wales. One prominent club in central Cardiff, a meeting place of senior private and public sector figures in Wales, refuses to allow women to become members. Freemasonry, which also excludes women, is thought to be particularly strong in Wales (the government's attempts to make knowledge about membership more public may show whether this is true). Elizabeth Muir, who was the first member of the Confederation of British Industry in Wales, has written of her experience of the 'otherness' of being a 'token' woman on an all-male board of directors (Muir 1994).

Conclusion

Patterns of segregation of men and women into different sectors and occupations are particularly rigid in Wales. This represents tremendous underutilization of women's skills and is economically inefficient. It contributes to Wales being a relatively low-wage economy. It is also one of the main explanations for the pay gap between men and women: jobs where the majority of incumbents are women appear automatically to be lower paid than similar jobs done by men. Why are these patterns so rigid? How do they reproduce themselves? One of the factors is that women and men tend to pursue different education and training trajectories. This is the subject of the next chapter.

4 Men's skills, women's talents

Education and training play a powerful role in the division of the workforce into male and female arenas. There have been considerable developments in the last twenty years, many of which have helped to reduce the impact of gender on who ultimately gets what jobs. However, at the same time, some of the checks and balances now built into the system of funding and provision have the effect of sustaining the gender divide. This chapter reports on the gendering of education and training in Wales and identifies some pointers for the future.

The EOC commissioned two studies which are highly pertinent to the concerns of this chapter. Salisbury (1996a) assessed the impact of various recent educational reforms on gender equality on schools in Wales. Women in post-compulsory education and training in Wales were the subject of an EOC-funded study published as a contribution to the work of Chwarae Teg (Istance and Rees 1994). Its tasks were to identify key aspects of the policy context, to provide a statistical review and to analyse special initiatives for women in education and training. These two studies among others are drawn upon here to provide an up-to-date picture of the gender dimension of education and training in Wales.

School-based education

Schools in Wales, as elsewhere, have experienced a series of changes since the 1970s, especially in recent years. The most significant of these was the Education Act of 1986, which gave governors a much more significant role and the Education Reform Act of 1988, which implemented the National Curriculum and introduced Standard Assessment Tests (SATs). More recent Acts have led to new systems of measuring performance of schools and, as a consequence, league tables.

To oversee and regulate this work, a range of bodies has been set up; some are on an England and Wales basis while others are specifically

Table 4.1: Examination achievements of pupils in schools, by region and sex, 1995/96 (percentages)

	2 or more GCE A levels[1]		5 or more GCSE grades A–C		No graded GCSEs[2]	
	Male	Female	Male	Female	Male	Female
England	19	21	40	49	9	7
Wales	18	23	37	47	12	9
Scotland	28	35	47	60	5	3
N. Ireland	26	37	45	59	7	3
United Kingdom	20	23	41	51	9	6

Source: Office of National Statistics (1998), *Social Trends*, London: The Stationery Office, Table 3.16. Original sources: DfEE, Welsh Office, Scottish Office Education and Industry Departments, Department of Education Northern Ireland.

Notes: [1]Pupils aged 17 to 19 at the end of the school year in England, Wales and Northern Ireland and as a percentage of the 18-year-old population. For Scotland the figures relate to pupils in years S5/S6 gaining 3 or more SCE Higher passes as a percentage of the 17-year-old population.
[2]Pupils aged 16 at the end of the school year as a percentage of the 15-year-old population at the start of the school year. Scotland pupils are in year S4.

Welsh institutions. In Salisbury's review of the impact of educational reforms on gender in Welsh schools, she alludes to the growing debate about how educational needs in Wales can best be served (Salisbury 1996a). To some, the mixture of autonomy in some areas and linkage to systems in England designed to serve a different context in others has led to a set of policies and practices that could be improved upon by an independent Welsh approach (see Bellin et al. 1994; Istance and Rees 1996; Reynolds 1995). The National Assembly of Wales provides the constitutional setting to facilitate the developments of policies more in tune with the specific needs of Wales, addressing the differences as well as the similarities with England.

Traditionally examination results in Wales have had a different pattern from those in England. There have been significant numbers of school leavers with good A-level results and, at the other end of the spectrum, large numbers with no qualifications at all. In England the general pattern has been a normal distribution, with the majority lying between these two extremes (see Rees and Rees 1980). Wales's lead at the well-qualified end has now been lost – indeed the proportion of leavers with two A levels is now lower than the British

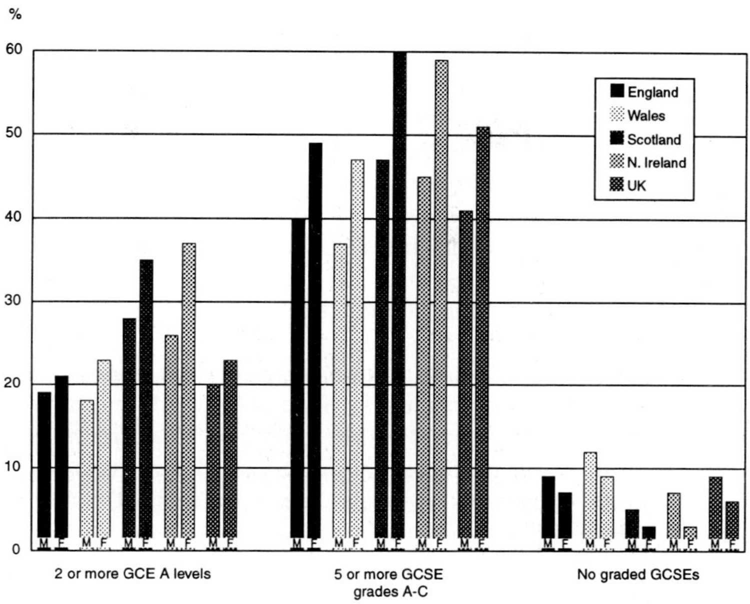

Figure 4.1 Examination achievements of pupils in schools by region and sex, 1995/96
Source: as Table 4.1.

average (see Table 4.1). Moreover, the numbers of unqualified leavers, while diminishing, remains high compared with other parts of the UK. Hence, some twenty-five years ago (1974/5), one in five young women (19.1 per cent) in Wales left school without any qualifications at all, compared with a quarter (24.5 per cent) of all young men. By 1984/5, these figures had dropped to 14.2 per cent and 18.9 per cent respectively (Central Statistical Office 1987: 96) and by 1995/6, to 9 per cent and 12 per cent – although still higher than the UK averages of 6 per cent and 9 per cent (Office for National Statistics 1998: Table 3.16). Rates of school-leavers entering the world of work with no qualifications at all are particularly high in the south Wales valleys communities. By contrast, in rural Wales, relatively few leave with no qualifications (Central Statistical Office 1995; Welsh Office 1995a).

Overall, the impact of the reforms on equal opportunities appears to have been mixed. One of the issues that has received most attention has been the fact that figures now show that girls have similar results to boys and, at some levels, do better than boys. This is not a particularly Welsh phenomenon: similar patterns can be found elsewhere (see, for example, Arnot et al.'s 1996 combined study of England and Wales). Indeed, the issue of 'underachieving boys' is being identified as a cause for concern in many European Union member states. Table 4.1 shows that fewer girls than boys have no graded GCSEs while more girls than boys achieve five or more GCSEs grades A to C.

The clear gender divide in subject choice is still a major issue and the result of this is to restrict the range of industries and occupations open to girls. This significant problem remains. This is despite the fact that the National Curriculum in effect obliges girls and boys to study subjects non-traditional for their gender up to a certain level. While many initiatives have been introduced which seek to promote gender quality in schools in Wales (see Daniel 1994), and to encourage more girls into non-traditional areas, for example science and engineering, for the most part they have been limited in their effects (Rees 1992).

Part of the explanation for this is found in young women's own views of their future. One study of 500 south Wales schoolgirls describes how the anticipation of a working life fragmented by child-care responsibilities inhibits an investment in education and training. Girls anticipate having to undertake part-time work to accommodate childcare needs and, given that part-time work is predominantly in unskilled or semi-skilled work, they are not then motivated to pursue qualifications (Pilcher et al. 1988; 1989a; 1989b; 1990; Rees 1992). Their subject and career choices are therefore heavily constrained. Startup and Dressel (1996) also find differences in the culture and aspirations of male and female secondary school pupils in Wales. Extraordinarily, Southall (1990), examining the aspirations of a group of young women fifth-form school-leavers in Cardiff in 1990, found that their hopes were highly circumscribed and differed little from the actual career trajectories of a group of women who had left the same school, aged fifteen, some fifteen years previously.

Work experience placements are now part of the National Curriculum. However, because in Wales they operate within a labour market that is particularly rigidly divided along gender lines, they can reinforce rather than challenge sex-stereotyped views young people may already have about gender-appropriate jobs by providing them

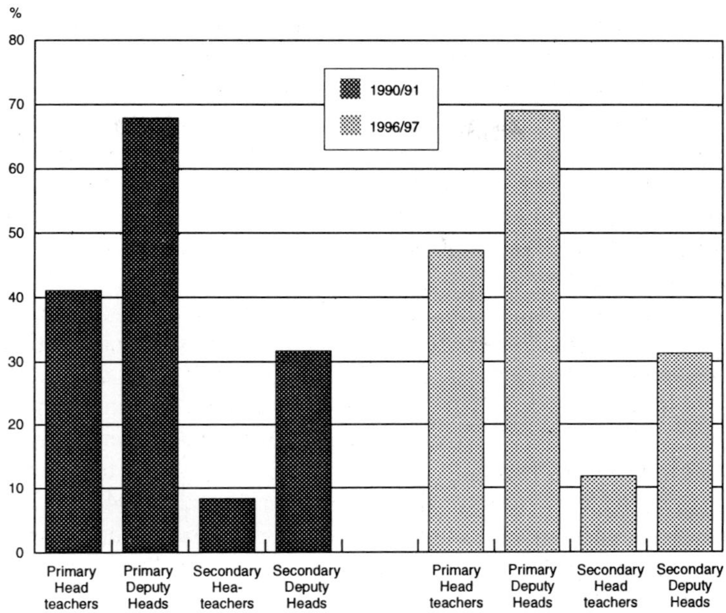

Figure 4.2 Percentage of women head teachers and deputy head teachers in Wales, 1990/91 and 1996/97
Source: as Table 4.2.

with first-hand experience of how men and women are valued differently in work. Teachers and careers officers in one study were concerned about the traditional choices being made by young women; some expressed particular worries about equal opportunities problems faced by young Asian pupils (Salisbury 1996b: 35).

In a major review of educational reforms in Wales, Salisbury found that while there appeared to be a commitment to equal opportunities from some individuals and groups in Welsh schools in the 1990s, the issue was not regarded as a high priority. Less than a fifth of primary and secondary schools' governing bodies 'were reported to be monitoring equal opportunities for teachers and pupils' (1996a: 34).

This is a matter of serious concern given that, in addition to the issues concerning pupils, the percentage of women head teachers in Wales is extremely small relative to the numbers of women in the profession. The proportion of women primary school heads has

Table 4.2: Women head teachers and deputy head teachers in Wales, 1990/91 and 1996/97

	1990/91		1996/97	
	No.	%	No.	%
Primary head teachers				
Men	1006	58.9	883	52.7
Women	703	41.1	795	47.3
Total	1709	100.0	1678	100.0
Primary deputy heads				
Men	439	32.1	395	30.9
Women	927	67.9	882	69.1
Total	1366	100.0	1277	100.0
Secondary head teachers				
Men	211	91.7	202	88.2
Women	19	8.3	27	11.8
Total	230	100.0	229	100.0
Secondary deputy heads				
Men	396	68.3	326	68.7
Women	184	31.7	149	31.3
Total	580	100.0	475	100.0

Source: Calculated from Welsh Office (1998), *Statistics of Education and Training in Wales: Schools 1997*, Cardiff: Welsh Office.

slowly increased during the 1990s, from 41.1 per cent in 1990/1 to 47.3 per cent in 1996/7, as has the percentage of women secondary school heads, from 8.3 per cent to 11.8 per cent over the same period. For both primary and secondary sectors, however, the percentage of deputies who are women has been declining over the decade, until a sudden upturn for women primary deputies in 1996/7 (see Table 4.2). Another way of looking at the statistics, which is perhaps more revealing, is to say that of all male primary school teachers in Wales in 1996/7, 54.9 per cent are either heads or deputies, compared with 17.5 per cent for women. Similarly, 9.0 per cent of all male secondary teachers are heads or deputies, compared with only 2.5 per cent of women secondary teachers (calculated from Welsh Office 1998a: Table 6.5). Over three-quarters of governing bodies in Wales, from whom members of appointment panels are drawn, have a male chair: this is a higher proportion than in England (Salisbury 1996a: 31).

A further significant area of change in Welsh school education over the last twenty years has been the extraordinary rise of Welsh-medium schools, particularly in south-east Wales. Many of the pupils come from monoglot English-speaking homes.

Post-compulsory education and training

There has been a rapid increase in staying-on rates in education, from half of all sixteen-year-olds in 1989 to 70 per cent in 1993. This is one of the contributors to the declining levels of economic activity in Wales and is characteristic of other parts of the UK too. Women stay on longer than men in the immediate post-sixteen period, especially in rural areas (Istance and Rees 1994).

Of greatest concern in the sixteen-to-eighteen-years age group is the fact that so many young people appear to be disappearing altogether from education, training and employment. In South Glamorgan, a research project revealed that up to a fifth of sixteen-to-eighteen-year-olds at any one time are not in education, training or employment: the 'disappeared' comprise about equal numbers of young men and women (Istance et al. 1994; G. Rees et al. 1996). They 'make out' in a number of ways including, in the case of some, involvement in crime and the black economy. The difficulties faced in seeking to draw such young people back into education and training systems are enormous.

The collapse of the youth labour market meant that less than 2 per cent of girls leaving school in 1993 went into a job with training (Careers Service Wales 1994). Women aged sixteen to nineteen are much less likely than men of the same age to be undertaking or to have completed apprenticeships (6 per cent compared with 13 per cent in 1994/5), and women apprentices are more likely to be in low-paid service-sector occupations such as hairdressing. A survey by the Welsh Office showed that 19 per cent of people of working age had completed or were undertaking a recognized trade apprenticeship in 1994/5; however, this figure was made up of a rate of 29 per cent for men and only 7 per cent of women (Welsh Office 1995a: 8). The percentage of men who have had apprenticeships has dropped from 35 per cent of 35-to-59-year-olds to the figure quoted earlier of 13 per cent for sixteen-to-nineteen-year-olds. For women, the figure of 7 per cent is constant for all age groups except sixteen-to-nineteen-year-olds where it drops to 6 per cent (see Table 4.3). There were spatial variations for men: high rates for men were recorded in Powys and north-west Wales, for example, but rates for women were fairly uniform across Wales with the exception of South Glamorgan (10 per cent). The England and Wales Youth Cohort Study of eighteen- and nineteen-year-olds found significant gender differences in job-related

Table 4.3: Persons who had completed, or were still doing, a recognized trade apprenticeship, by sex and age in Wales,[1] 1994/95 (percentage)

	Male	Female	Persons
16–19	13	6	9
20–24	20	7	14
25–34	25	7	16
35–49	35	7	21
50–59	35	7	21
60–64	30	–	30
Total	29	7	19

Source: Welsh Office (1995), *1994/5 Welsh Training and Education Survey*, Cardiff: Welsh Office.

Note: [1]Persons of working age.

training. Women were three times more likely to have just a one- or two-day induction course (15 per cent of women compared with 5 per cent of men) whereas 48 per cent of men expected their training to last two years or more compared with 29 per cent of women (Park 1994).

Women are keen consumers of post-school education opportunities but are more likely to pursue academic than vocational training courses (Istance and Rees 1994). They constitute 76 per cent of enrolments in adult education classes run by local authorities (Welsh Office 1997: Table 3.7) and form the majority of further education students, but they are more frequently found in evening classes and among self-funded students rather than employer-sponsored students on day or block release. Two-thirds of students with 'day-release arrangements' are men (Istance and Rees 1994). Women have been less likely to end up with qualifications as a result of their studies; however, this may change as alterations in funding arrangements mean that such courses are more likely to become certificated in the future (although the likely effect of this on participation patterns is unknown). As a consequence of these trends, women's knowledge and skills are less recognized and rewarded by the labour market, hence they are likely to be employed at a level below their potential.

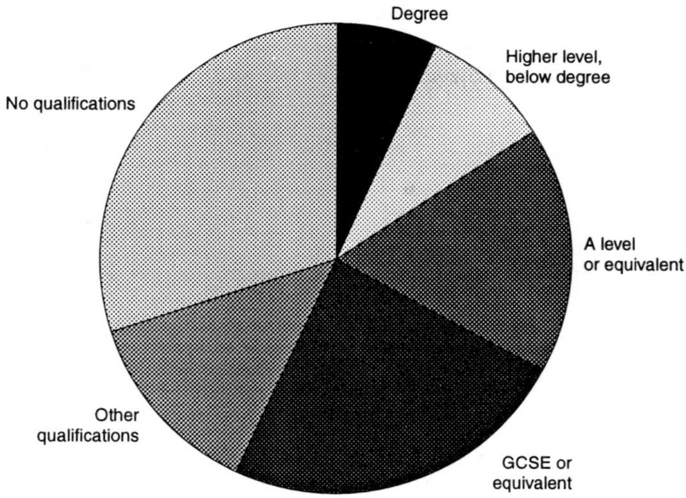

Figure 4.3a Highest qualifications held in Wales by sex, 1994/95 (females)
Source: as Table 4.4.

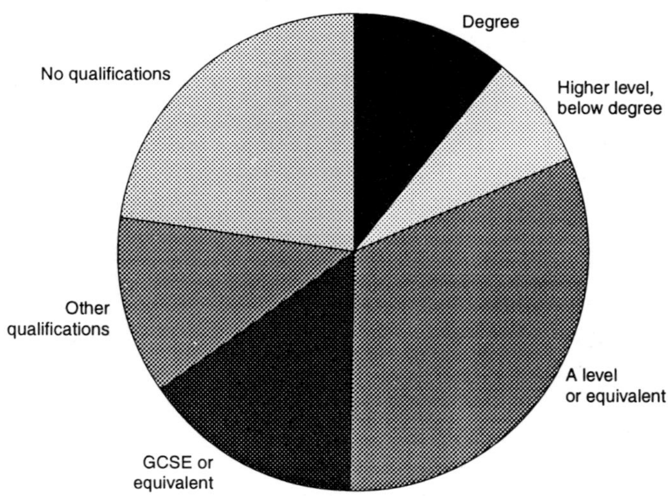

Figure 4.3b Highest qualifications held in Wales by sex, 1994/95 (males)
Source: as Table 4.4.

Table 4.4: Highest qualification held in Wales by TEC area and sex,[1] 1994/95 (percentage)

	Gwent	Mid Glamorgan	North East Wales	North West Wales	Powys	South Glamorgan	West Wales	Wales
Males								
Degree	10	6	10	8	11	18	13	11
Higher level, below degree	6	8	9	9	6	7	9	8
A level or equivalent	30	30	34	36	31	33	30	32
GCSE or equivalent	14	15	16	15	14	15	15	15
Other qualifications	14	14	10	8	11	10	11	12
No qualifications	25	27	22	25	28	17	22	23
Total	100	100	100	100	100	100	100	100
Females								
Degree	6	5	5	6	7	15	8	7
Higher level, below degree	9	8	11	11	11	9	10	9
A level or equivalent	13	17	17	15	18	19	18	17
GCSE or equivalent	25	24	29	27	21	19	22	24
Other qualifications	12	14	10	12	13	13	14	13
No qualifications	36	33	28	30	29	26	29	30
Total	100	100	100	100	100	100	100	100
Persons								
Degree	8	6	8	7	9	16	11	9
Higher level, below degree	8	8	10	10	8	8	9	9
A level or equivalent	22	24	26	26	25	26	24	24
GCSE or equivalent	19	19	22	21	17	17	18	19
Other qualifications	13	14	10	10	12	11	12	12
No qualifications	30	30	25	27	29	21	26	27
Total	100	100	100	100	100	100	100	100

Source: Welsh Office (1995), *1994/5 Welsh Training and Education Survey*, Cardiff: Welsh Office.

Note: [1]Persons of working age.

Figures do not always appear to total 100 because of rounding.

Table 4.5: Highest qualification held in Wales by age and sex,[1] 1994/95 (percentage)

	16–19	20–24	25–34	35–49	50–59	60–64	Total
Males							
Degree	–	11	12	14	9	8	11
Higher level, below degree	–	5	10	10	6	7	8
A level or equivalent	20	38	29	34	33	28	32
GCSE or equivalent	43	21	18	10	7	4	15
Other qualifications	13	12	14	12	8	10	12
No qualifications	23	14	17	19	36	43	23
Total	100	100	100	100	100	100	100
Females							
Degree	–	8	11	8	5	–	7
Higher level, below degree	–	7	9	12	9	–	9
A level or equivalent	20	30	18	15	10	–	17
GCSE or equivalent	45	29	28	21	11	–	24
Other qualifications	13	13	13	11	13	–	13
No qualifications	21	14	21	33	51	–	30
Total	100	100	100	100	100	–	100
Persons							
Degree	–	9	12	11	7	8	9
Higher level, below degree	–	6	10	11	8	7	9
A level or equivalent	20	34	23	24	22	28	24
GCSE or equivalent	44	25	23	16	9	4	19
Other qualifications	13	12	13	12	11	10	12
No qualifications	22	14	19	26	44	43	27
Total	100	100	100	100	100	100	100

Source: Welsh Office (1995), *1994/5 Welsh Training and Education Survey*, Cardiff: Welsh Office.

Note: [1]Persons of working age.
Figures do not always appear to total 100 because of rounding.

Underemployment is a major issue for women in Wales, and for the Welsh economy.

Women are outnumbered by men in non-university higher education. There is a strong gender divide in subject choice in this sector. Again, men are more likely to follow sandwich and release courses. Women now constitute about half the university student population at undergraduate level but are found in smaller numbers than men at the postgraduate level (44 per cent in 1992). Again, gender is a strong determinant of subject choice. Welsh women are under-represented in science, technology and engineering – all growth areas in the economy (Istance and Rees 1994).

The highest qualifications held by men and women in Wales in the training and enterprise council (TEC) areas are set out in Table 4.4 which comes from an enhanced *Labour Force Survey* published by the Welsh Office (1995a). It shows that men are much better qualified than women. However, the increased staying on rates of women in education mean that the gap is much narrower in the younger age groups than among older people of working age: this is highlighted in Table 4.5. Moreover, universities and colleges, in the face of an ageing population, are increasingly keen to recruit mature-age students and women have responded to these opportunities with both enthusiasm and trepidation, as the next section shows.

Overall gender segregation in post-compulsory education and training still exists and women lose out in particular in employer-sponsored training. This is partly a structural problem: they tend not to be found in those industries or in those technical and managerial grades where most of such sponsorship occurs. However, at the same time women now constitute about half the university student population, especially in those degree courses that lead to professions such as law and medicine. Overall, the major problem of gender segregation by subject in education and training remains.

Mature-age students

The number of access students expanded tenfold in Wales between 1988/9 and 1993/4. Since three-quarters of access students then go on to higher education courses and women constitute 58 per cent of access students (Istance and Rees 1994), these courses have made a significant impact on women's levels of participation in higher education.

To what extent have mainstream higher education providers adapted to the needs of mature students who now comprise a growing proportion of the student body? Accessing mainstream education and training provision, when it may not be designed with the needs of your sex or age group in mind can certainly be very daunting (Betts et al. 1995; Garland 1992; Lodge et al. 1991). Garland describes the difficulties faced by women returners to higher education in north Wales and, also, how they felt empowered when they perceived themselves differently as a result of their new identity. As one of Garland's respondents reports: 'I stood up for myself more, I realised my point of view was as important as anyone else's. I didn't take kindly to being put down, in that sense I did gain confidence' (Garland 1994: 119).

A study of gender and participation in adult education in Wales (Francis et al. 1996) found that women outnumber men by 3:2 in university-based adult continuing education in Wales. Access and vocational courses, the humanities, Welsh for adults and courses based in the community tended to have higher percentages of female students (p.8). As we saw in schools, however, while all the departments in this study had an equal opportunities policy, either at the departmental or institutional level, the 'strategies to ensure equality of opportunity for men and women in relation to access to provision, delivery methods and support facilities are of variable quality' (Francis et al. 1996: 8).

Job-related training

It is in job-related training in Wales that some of the widest gender gaps persist. In the early 1990s, the government set National Training and Education Targets (NTETs): Foundation Targets were set for young people to achieve National Vocational Qualification (NVQ) Levels 2 and 3 or their equivalent and Lifetime Targets were established for adults in the workforce to achieve NVQs or units towards them (LT2) and NVQ3 or equivalent (LT3).

Wales started from a low base in terms of NTETs for the proportion of the working population with qualifications of both different levels and has been slower to progress than other regions (Istance and G. Rees 1995; Istance and T. Rees 1996). Moreover, Felstead (1996b) analysed Spring 1994 *Labour Force Survey* data by gender and showed that the gender gap in Wales was 8.88 per cent (25.37 per cent of men compared with 16.49 per cent of women had Lifetime Target 1 level). This is bigger than the gap in Northern Ireland (5.62 per cent) and England (7.66 per cent), but smaller than that for Scotland (9.76 per cent).

The Welsh Office survey revealed that 5 per cent of the people of working age questioned reported that they had a NVQ. However, 7 per cent had never heard of them or did not know whether they had

Table 4.6: Persons achieving NVQ level 3 or equivalent in Wales, by sex,[1] 1994/95 (percentage)

	Males	Females	Persons
Gwent	44	29	37
Mid Glamorgan	42	29	36
North East Wales	44	32	38
North West Wales	40	32	37
Powys	38	33	36
South Glamorgan	53	45	49
West Wales	44	35	40
Wales	44	34	39

Source: Welsh Office (1995), *1994/5 Welsh Training and Education Survey*, Cardiff: Welsh Office.
Note: [1]Persons in the workforce.

one. Of those who reported that they did have an NVQ, around equal numbers of men and women held them at levels 1 and 2, but 58 per cent of the higher-level NVQs were held by men. Overall, the survey reports, men held 54 per cent of NVQs and women 46 per cent (Welsh Office 1995a: 9).

Table 4.6 shows the spatial distribution of people achieving NVQ level 3 or equivalent by sex. It shows that South Glamorgan has the highest proportions of men and women with these qualifications, followed by west Wales. A third of women have reached this level compared with 44 per cent of men. The *Labour Force Survey* shows that the proportion of employees in Wales who received job-related training in the month leading up to the survey (13.4 per cent) was one of the lowest of any of the British regions and below the British average (14.5 per cent). Moreover, the proportion of women reporting job-related training is lower in Wales than all the other regions at 12.5 per cent; only men in the East Midlands recorded a lower score (Istance and Rees 1996).

Of particular concern is the lack of opportunities for training for part-time workers, the vast majority of whom are women. McGiveney (1994) reports on the 'wasted potential' this represents. Women working part time now contribute a quarter of the Welsh workforce, so this omission is a serious issue.

The rise in credentialism

Many professions are characterized by an increasing credentialism. This has had a beneficial effect for women as it has made transparent what is required for entry to the professions (Crompton and Sanderson 1986). The increase in women entering careers such as law, accountancy and professions allied to medicine is noticeable. The rising demand for qualifications in management is particularly significant here too, especially in the health service and in further education, both of which are major employers of women. This means that people already in employment may have to seek further qualifications in order simply to continue to do the same job.

Salisbury (1994) describes a group of women and men who undertook in-service training as further education lecturers. Such new challenges can undermine confidence at the time. However, as Salisbury reports, opportunities for in-service training can be highly beneficial to women. As one of her respondents, an ex-hairdresser (in the classic 'educating Rita' style) who is now a further education lecturer, has said:

> I can now say I've been to university! [laughter] I had to work hard but it worked. I've got a teaching certificate now, so no HMI [Her Majesty's Inspectorate] can embarrass me again by asking if I'm qualified. I'm a proper teacher with a proper certificate!
>
> ('Alice Bristow', quoted in Salisbury 1994: 158)

Additional qualifications and enhanced standards of professionalism are increasingly required in a wide range of occupations and professions. Women's access to such opportunities is therefore vital. For women who are working full time and may be more likely to have to spend a greater proportion of their non-working hours on domestic responsibilities, such educational imperatives can be difficult to find the time to meet. This is an issue discussed in chapter 5 on the balance between home and work.

'Sisters are doing it for themselves': women's training initiatives in Wales

Mainstream training provision for initial and continuing training is beginning to take on board the needs of women but, as the participation figures show, only at certain levels and in a relatively narrow range of subjects. And those who do gain these qualifications are not always rewarded by being appointed to appropriate jobs. It is partly in response to this that a series of initiatives has developed in Wales which seek to provide training more geared to women's needs in all their diversity. Some have the accolade of being regarded by the European Commission as 'model projects'. Nevertheless, their funding remains piecemeal and uncertain and they are outside mainstream provision.

Probably the best-known example is the South Glamorgan Women's Workshop (SGWW), which recently celebrated its tenth anniversary. In the late 1980s a group of women in Cardiff recognized that mainstream training providers did not accommodate the needs of unqualified, disadvantaged women wanting to return to the labour market. With extraordinary tenacity and hard work, and with the backing of South Glamorgan County Council, they succeeded in securing funding from the European Commission and other sources to set up the SGWW in order to train women returners in computing and other skills (Essex et al. 1986; Rees 1993, 1994b). It has since moved into new premises in Cardiff Bay which include a nursery on the ground floor and a room for prayers for Muslim women on the top floor. As the testimony of many of the women who have moved through the workshop and on to other education, training and employment opportunities has shown, the Workshop filled a real need (MacNamara 1990).

The Dove Workshop in Banwen was set up by women who had come together through miners' support groups during the 1984/5 strike. It has also received backing from local authorities, notably Onllwyn, and has developed links with other women's projects in ex-mining regions elsewhere in Europe. Along with the SGWW, it has been recognized as a model project by IRIS, the European Network of Women's Training Workshops (see Pudner and Francis 1994). Courses for women in rural Dyfed have also participated in European networking activities (Venus 1994). Chwarae Teg (1996d) has documented four less well-known projects in Wales for the European Commission, and the EOC and Chwarae Teg together have published a handbook on 'how education can help women achieve success in finding employment, developing careers, starting businesses or progressing to further and higher education', drawing on the experiences of positive-action projects (EOC/Chwarae Teg 1993: 3).

Local authorities have been crucial in supporting such women's initiatives. South Glamorgan County Council set up a Women Returners' Unit and Powys County Council has supported a number of New Opportunities for Women (NOW) projects. Gwent, too, has been involved in projects for women aimed at fostering women's enterprise and technological skills. It is too early to judge what impact local government reorganization into new unitary authorities will have on support available for crucial initiatives of this kind.

Participation in European co-funded training

An increasing number of training providers is accessing European sources to co-fund training, some of which is aimed exclusively at women or from which women benefit. The SGWW and the Dove Workshop have been mentioned, but further education colleges, universities and organizations such as the Workers' Educational Association have also accessed European Social Funds or monies from the NOW strand of the European Commission's Employment Initiative to provide women-only courses, for example, in parenting skills, with crèche facilities provided. These can operate effectively as a first stage in returning to learning, an affordable or free stepping stone to access courses where funding arrangements now increasingly insist upon students enrolling for credited courses: a daunting prospect for those with eroded confidence.

The European Affairs Department of the Welsh Development Agency (WDA) has been proactive in co-ordinating European partnerships, some of which explore aspects of women's training needs (see WDA 1993a). The Athena project looked at skills, training and women's economic development, focusing on barriers to women's training in six regions of the European Union (Rees 1994c). The team in Wales looked particularly at the training needs of women seeking to become self-employed or set up their own business. Drawing on research with existing women entrepreneurs, a series of recommendations emanated from the project, one of which for Wales was that enterprise agencies needed to be more alert to specific training and support needs of women (WDA 1993b). This led ultimately to a further European co-funded project under the 'Leonardo da Vinci' action programme on training, called Diva. The end product of this project was a video aimed at enterprise agencies, illustrating the need to widen their client base and to 'realise diversity'. A further WDA co-ordinated project examined the training needs of women employees in regions of four member states (Dublin in Ireland, Catalonia in Spain, Thessaloniki in Greece and Wales in the UK). The Axia project, as it was known (Axia being Greek for value), demonstrated the value of transnational learning in identifying women's training needs and how conventional providers fell short of meeting them. It provided some concrete lessons (Rees 1994d; 1995a).

During the 1990s, more 'spaces' for women's education and training projects have been created by the European Commission through earmarked funds in an attempt to foster positive-action projects to combat women's disadvantaged position in the labour market and address the issue of low skills. However, in the late 1990s this approach is being complemented by one of 'mainstreaming' equal opportunities within the Structural Funds (including the European Social Fund) and 'Leonardo da Vinci' (see Rees 1994e; 1998). This approach and its potential impact is discussed in the final chapter.

Funding Councils and Training and Enterprise Councils

In an earlier section, we saw how, although women are the majority of teachers in Wales, they are considerably less likely than men to become head teachers. The further and higher education sectors too are highly male dominated. It is worth noting here that the Further Education Funding Council has a male chair and chief executive, and one woman among its eight council members. The Higher Education Funding Council also has a male chair, and shares its chief executive with the Further Education Funding Council. It has one woman on its seven-person board. The Council of Welsh TECs has a male chair and chief executive, and no women members or chief officers. There are no women chairs or chief executives at any of the six Welsh TECs, and only ten women among the seventy-five board members (13.3 per cent) (all figures from Balsom 1997). This 'political arithmetic' exercise demonstrates a clear lack of female representation in the decision-making processes leading to the funding and shaping of further and higher education.

Conclusion

Clearly, there is a symbiotic relationship between the industrial structure of Wales and patterns of participation in post-compulsory education and training: the two are interdependent. But, as some commentators have warned, there is a danger that Wales will consolidate its image as a low-skill, low-wage economy, attractive to inward investors but unlikely to 'grow' skilled jobs with higher wages. The particular set of institutional arrangements in Wales and the focus that will be provided by the Welsh Assembly, together with potential initiatives flagged up in the Welsh Office *Lifelong Learning* Green Paper (Welsh Office 1998b) creates an opportunity to reverse this downward spiral. However, it is vital to address the gender dimension of education and training. As the figures in this chapter show, there is huge underdevelopment and underutilization of women's potential and actual skills and qualifications. Unless this is faced in an active rather than *laissez faire* way, the Welsh economy's future looks set to depend upon the fortunes of the service sector and the decisions of inward investors.

5 Balancing home and work

If women are more likely to be undertaking paid work in the 1990s compared with the 1970s, does this mean that men are more likely to be sharing domestic work? What evidence there is suggests not. The consequence for women tends to be a 'choice' between part-time work or, in some cases, becoming very overburdened. Encouraging a saner balance of home and work, to the benefit of families and employers as well as employees and family members, is high on the agenda of the European Commission (1994). Unfortunately it is an issue that appears to receive little attention in the UK more generally or in Wales specifically, although it could be argued that there are many reasons why the debate is of particular pertinence here.

The UK is out on a limb in a number of ways: men work longer hours than men in all the other EU member states, we have fewer holidays, and there is less pre-school childcare provision. Getting a balance between home and working life is seen by the European Commission as essential to creating a healthy and effective working environment. Involvement in non-work activities is recognized as providing opportunities for employees to gain experiences and learn skills from which the employer can benefit. Moreover, the fact that the UK has a long-hours culture is not linked to a higher gross domestic product than other member states or to the production of better-quality goods and services. We appear to be locked into a self-perpetuating culture which values hours worked and visibility ('presenteeism') over effectiveness. How does this culture impact upon men and women's lives in Wales?

This chapter takes a different slant on twenty-five years of women in the workforce by examining this issue of the balance between home and work. It focuses on three themes: the domestic division of labour, family-friendly employment policies and childcare facilities in Wales. In reviewing the last twenty-five years under these three headings, it is clear that there has been both change and continuity. As we saw in chapter 2, men's wages have diminished in real terms as a result of patterns of industrial restructuring, and as male economic activity rates have declined, so more women are entering the workforce. There may be more childcare provision than there was, and more employers have sought to introduce family-friendly policies which help women to combine their two roles. However, as women's wages are for the most part low, some of their wages are vital simply to keep family incomes above the poverty line. This means that in the absence of subsidized childcare, private provision can prove to be too costly. As a consequence, many women have to make a complex set of arrangements with friends and family, including husbands or partners, to meet child-care needs.

The first question, then, relates to the domestic division of labour. Are men more likely to be contributing to housework and caring responsibilities at the turn of the century? Have there been any sightings of the 'new man' in Wales? It is of course very difficult to find out what happens in families behind closed doors: the next section draws together some of the scant evidence we have in Wales on this matter.

Domestic division of labour

A series of studies by the Welsh Development Agency (WDA) as a contribution to the work of Chwarae Teg in the early 1990s found that over half the women outside the labour market identified family responsibilities as the main barrier to undertaking training before returning to work (Rees and Willox 1991a; 1991b; Willox 1992). A follow-up study in 1996 found that 44 per cent of non-economically active women reported that their reason for not working was that it was too difficult to combine a job with children (ERES 1996: 92).

While the main issue cited was childcare, in an ageing society, care for the elderly is now increasingly a factor too. Wenger (1994) has described the significance of family and friends in determining the kinds of care arrangements and level of independence enjoyed by elderly women in north Wales. As we saw in chapter 2, Wales has a high level of long-term limiting sickness and disability: this again means that many women of working age are caring for relatives who are neither children nor elderly. Indeed, ERES found that some women themselves reporting such a condition were nevertheless caring for others (ERES 1994). Given that there is less childcare provision in the UK than in all but one of the other fifteen member states of the EU and that Wales already has a demographic structure and health profile that demands a considerable amount of support for others, it is clear that women's ability to participate in the labour force will be severely curtailed unless men make a significant contribution to this caring work.

We have two sources of information on the domestic division of labour in Wales, one from the 1970s and one from the 1990s which give us some indication of change over time. A study of the division of domestic work between adults in the home in the Swansea area in the 1970s described it in the following terms:

> Almost all the daily domestic houseworking is done by the wife/mother – the cooking, cleaning and tidying, washing and ironing, bedmaking, sewing and shopping. The husband/father in South Wales may make and tend the fire, and he will do occasional work like painting and decorating, some house-hold repairs, and car maintenance. Either husband or wife will look after the garden, though allotments, if taken on, are almost exclusively male preserves. In addition the husband may 'give his wife a hand' with the washing up, and he may drive her to the shops and carry home the purchases on a Saturday, particularly if she has a job. But men almost never take care of (i.e. feed or change) babies or small children within the house, though they may 'keep an eye' on them and take them out for walks.
>
> (Leonard 1980: 57)

Jenkins and Hutson report on changes from the patterns in the late 1970s described by Leonard in their study of the late 1980s:

> More to the point perhaps is the importance of social change with respect to women's consciousness: the redefinition of gender roles with respect to employment and the family, and, more generally, attitudes towards sexuality and its expression. This, of course, is not to paint a picture of a revolution in gender equality achieved, but simply to say some changes have occurred.
>
> (Jenkins and Hutson 1990: 114)

This redefinition of gender roles is a key issue that is found in other studies. Changes in ideas about who has responsibility for various household tasks and who 'helps' in their execution is highlighted in a fascinating study by Pilcher (1994). She examines Welsh women from three generations (grandmothers, their daughters and their grown-up granddaughters) talking about their husbands and domestic work. She notes a shift in the vocabularies used, from the grandmothers 'owning' the domestic work to the mothers 'expecting some help', to the granddaughters (many of whom, it has to be said, were not yet living with a partner) expecting housework to be 'shared'. Pilcher found that for the grandmothers an important part of their identity was rooted in their being responsible for the home and the children. However, she concludes that for the youngest generation of Welsh women, 'feminine identities are less bound up with notions of exclusive female domestic roles than is the case for older women' (1994: 32).

These indications suggest that there may be a change of expectation on the part of young women, but there is little evidence of changes in the division of labour itself. Moreover, Campbell's study of Britain's 'dangerous places', which included some very disadvantaged south Wales communities, looks at young disaffected men, fathers of babies born to teenage girls, living in a culture of booze and joy-riding. It offers little indication of a new domestic order there:

> According to a youth worker . . . their culture was about 'proving themselves by having bottle, being good drivers, getting into places, looking for fights all the time, being a bit crazier than everybody else, being able to get control of other people'.
>
> Another community worker reckoned that 'by the time the lasses have the kids the lads are twiddling their thumbs. They just walk away from it. I've seen it happen for years. They never take responsibility . . .'
>
> (Campbell 1993: 201)

Research into the situation in Britain as a whole (Bagihole 1994; Gershuny et al. 1986; Opportunity 2000 1994) suggests that while men may help more, most tasks are still regarded as the responsibility of women, even when they join or return to the workforce and even when they work full time. Part-time women workers (of whom there are particularly high rates in Wales) fare worse than women who work full time.

Family-friendly policies

Many employers have sought to accommodate the other demands on women workers by making adaptations to the organization of work.

Such policies include workplace nurseries, flexitime, career-break schemes, returner schemes including induction and refresher training, part-time houfs, term-time contracts, job-sharing and working from home. Of all of these in Wales, it is part-time working that is the most widespread (see chapter 2).

Organizations such as Chwarae Teg, Opportunity 2000 and the EOC's Equality Exchange have provided advice, support and information for employers interested in these measures. Chwarae Teg has produced a *Carers in Work Guide* aimed at employers, describing ways in which employers can provide the flexibility to enable employees to undertake their caring responsibilities for adult sick and disabled relatives (Chwarae Teg and Carers National Association 1996). It is often larger employers who have the flexibility to make most progress in introducing such measures. Unfortunately, some of the major public and private sector employers which have made greatest progress in these approaches are in sectors which have faced retrenchment. This has inevitably impacted upon the extent to which these arrangements are continued.

The EOC commissioned a major piece of work on the economics of equal opportunities which includes the accounts of major companies and small and medium-sized enterprises that have adopted family-friendly working (Humphries and Rubery 1996). In Wales, there has been a number of initiatives designed to address this issue. The National Health Service in Wales has produced a guide to flexible working practices (NHS Cymru 1993) which addresses the long-hours culture issue and Chwarae Teg (1996a) held a conference on the business benefits of family-friendly working. As yet, however, part-time work remains the main approach adopted in Wales to accommodating workers' family lives, and the long-hours culture, which causes so many difficulties in achieving a balanced life, appears to remain unchallenged.

Childcare

It is difficult to estimate how long basic tasks associated with childcare take a family in any given week, but one estimate calculates a figure of fifty hours a week (Piachaud 1985). Little is known about who performs these tasks or provides more general childcare in Wales. This is because there is a complex web of patterns of provision involving private arrangements, statutory provision and private and voluntary sector care.

There have been a number of significant changes in recent years in the field of childcare. The Children's Act of 1989 obliges local authorities to give an account of childcare facilities which gives more of a picture than has been available before. However, a Department of Employment study of 5,500 women in Britain in the early 1980s found that 40 per cent of pre-school children were cared for by grandmothers, with fathers providing care for a further 13 per cent (Martin and Roberts 1984). In Wales, only 9 per cent of parents of school-age children use paid childcare (Hanney et al. 1993), hence audits of childcare facilities, while essential, cannot give the full picture (Ashton 1994b).

Demand for childcare has certainly risen. In chapter 1 we saw that there was a growth in one-parent families in Wales and that many more mothers, both with partners and without, now participate in or wish to take up paid work. The WDA studies indicating the hidden need for childcare facilities from women intending to return to work were the first real indication of the potential level of unmet demand (Rees and Willox 1991a; 1991b; Willox 1992). This has been confirmed by a later study which showed that of unemployed women in Wales, 28 per cent considered the unavailability of childcare a barrier to their employment and 34 per cent thought the wages from a job would be unlikely to cover the costs of childcare (ERES 1996).

Recent research includes a survey of women in employment, in the home, in training and registered unemployed. This revealed that 55 per cent of employed women used a relative or friend (unpaid) to care for their pre-school children, though 21 per cent of women working full-time used a private nursery (ERES 1996: iv). A further point of note is the 46 per cent of women working part time who reported that they were either the chief or joint wage-earner in the family (19 per cent were the sole earner) and that their main motivation to work was financial. The assumption that women working part time provide supplementary wages to a household is therefore not grounded in fact. The affordability of childcare is a crucial issue if women are to be able to take up opportunities for education and training and move out of ghettoized low-waged, part-time work, unemployment, non-employment and under-employment. It is significant that the economic activity rate for married mothers in Wales is higher than that of single mothers and is lower among mothers with no qualifications who are less likely to be able to afford childcare.

A childcare audit commissioned by Chwarae Teg in 1996 drew attention to a number of recent policy developments (Stratham et al. 1996). At a GB level, a pre-school education voucher scheme for four-year-olds was set up by the Conservative government in the mid-1990s, but, while welcome in principle, it proved inappropriate to the situation in Wales where children start school a year earlier than in England. Similarly a 'childcare disregard' in family credit was introduced in 1995 but was found to be difficult to put into operation. Specifically in Wales there was government support for the start-up of out-of-school care (through the TECs' Out of School Childcare Initiative) and the setting up of Welsh-Office-funded Childcare Demonstration Projects for the under-fives (Chwarae Teg 1996b; 1996c). These aim to involve employers in new childcare projects and were launched following the publications of *People and Prosperity: An Agenda for Action* (Welsh Office 1995b).

Both the audit and the Welsh Office under-fives initiative were highlighted in a recent DfEE/Scottish Office/Welsh Office (1996) consultation paper *Work and Family*; the current Labour government has given a higher priority to childcare and the balance between work and family life than the previous Conservative one.

Childcare provision in Wales remains at a level lower than that of England. Nevertheless, Stratham et al. (1996) found a growth in the number of private day nursery places since the first childcare audit conducted for Chwarae Teg in 1993 (see Table 5.1) (Hanney et al. 1993). The number of places with childminders and out-of-school clubs has also risen. The increase has come from the independent sector rather than the public sector. While much of the attention focuses on pre-school needs, and now to an extent after-school hours, it can be more difficult to address needs during half-terms and school holidays, and when children are sick.

Despite these developments, targets set by Chwarae Teg in the 1993 audit have not been reached. The issue of affordability is clearly linked to women's low wages. Employers still seem reluctant to support childcare. Chwarae Teg produced a document *Good Childcare, Better Business* (1993) which was followed up with seminars for employers and training providers, arguing the business case. An expansion in childcare facilities provided by colleges and universities was identified in the childcare audit (Stratham et al. 1996). The voluntary sector plays a crucial role. Mudiad Ysgolion Meithrin makes a significant contribution to childcare in Wales; set up in 1971,

Table 5.1: Change in the number of childcare services between 1992/93 and 1995/96, by county

	1992/93	1995/96	% change
Clywd			
Childminders	516	458	–11
Day nurseries	56	64	+14
Out-of-school clubs	24	47	+96
Dyfed			
Childminders	141	333	+136
Day nurseries	17	34	+100
Out-of-school clubs	2	17	+750
Gwent			
Childminders	489	607	+24
Day nurseries	16	23	+44
Out-of-school clubs	n/a	10	n/a
Gwynedd			
Childminders	251	300	+20
Day nurseries	15	19	+27
Out-of-school clubs	1	9	+800
Mid Glamorgan			
Childminders	687	783	+14
Day nurseries	15	19	+33
Out-of-school clubs	n/a	9	n/a
Powys			
Childminders	137	217	+58
Day nurseries	15	20	+33
Out-of-school clubs	2	4	+100
South Glamorgan			
Childminders	622	928	+49
Day nurseries	61	70	+15
Out-of-school clubs	n/a	34	n/a
West Glamorgan			
Childminders	243	368	+51
Day nurseries	18	22	+22
Out-of-school clubs	3	9	+200
Wales			
Childminders	3086	3994	+29
Day nurseries	213	272	+27
Out-of-school clubs	n/a	139	n/a

Source: J. Stratham et al. (1996), *Childcare in Wales: The 1996 Audit*, Cardiff: Chwarae Teg (Table 3).
Original source of 1992/3 figures is the first Audit of Childcare in Wales, updated where necessary from 1993 Day Care Reviews. Source of 1995/6 figures is the 1996 Day Care Review where available, otherwise statistics supplied by social services from list of registered providers. Figures for Gwent, Mid Glamorgan, South Glamorgan and West Glamorgan refer to summer or autumn 1995, for the other four counties to March 1996.

it runs Welsh-medium pre-school playgroups. However, in the voluntary sector generally, funding is always precarious. The authors of the audit conclude that a childcare strategy is badly needed.

Chwarae Teg has been working with a number of employers to seek partnership arrangements in childcare provision (Chwarae Teg 1996b; 1996c). Childcare facilities are expensive to set up and it is vital to know whether there is likely to be sufficient demand. Local audits of demand and supply can be useful in assessing likely usage. A partnership arrangement can offer advantages to employers and employees, both in terms of shared cost and in offering flexibility to accommodate varying levels of demand year by year.

Provision of childcare remains uneven in different areas of Wales, and is of course particularly problematic in rural Wales (see Ashton 1994b). Table 5.1 gives some indication of the change in numbers of childcare services (childminders, day nurseries and out-of-school clubs) in Wales by old county from 1992/3 to 1995/6. While there is a general pattern of increase in provision, it is from a very low base. The Chwarae Teg Wales Childcare Information Service is a bilingual computerized database of childcare facilities for the whole of Wales to assist parents in finding appropriate local care. It can be accessed at places such as Jobcentres and libraries and is used by adult guidance workers (Chwarae Teg 1996d). The information stored in the database reflects the unevenness of provision.

It is clear that quality of care is very important for parents entrusting their children to others. The measurement of quality in childcare has become an issue in recent years in response to the government policy of certificating skills. It was a Welsh company, Acorn Nurseries, which was the first in Europe to receive a quality Kitemark for standard of quality in childcare. Powys now has an Early Years National Vocational Qualifications Assessment Centre, supported by Powys TEC, where candidates can be trained to NVQ level 3 in Child Care and Education and Play Work: this is one of the places where childcare workers can be awarded a qualification for those skills (see Chwarae Teg 1996b). Degree courses in early childcare studies represent one of the fastest growth areas in universities.

The *Childcare in Wales* audit demonstrates the need for a childcare strategy for Wales. The authors argue that this would

> bring together the public, private and voluntary sectors in planning a programme of investment in childcare services for under fives and school

> aged children. It would recognise the importance of childcare in economic and social regeneration, and work towards making high quality, affordable childcare services available to all families in Wales.
>
> (Stratham et al. 1996)

This call for a strategic approach to childcare is being fed back to DfEE and Welsh Office in response to their consultative document on childcare (DfEE/Scottish Office/Welsh Office 1996). The fact that there is now such a debate taking place represents a significant step forward. The UK government has also signed up to the EC's Parental Leave Directive which will be implemented, following consultation, by December 1999. It will require the introduction of a minimum of three months' leave for working mothers and fathers (natural and adoptive), to be taken before the child is eight years old, and introduce an annual entitlement for working parents to family leave in cases of sickness or accident. Key issues such as whether the leave should be paid or unpaid are yet to be resolved.

Conclusion

Despite these initiatives and developments, and the commitments of the current government to a childcare strategy and encouraging lone mothers back to work, childcare and care for the disabled, sick and elderly remain significant issues in Wales in balancing home and work. There are indications that the large public and private sector employers are interested in family-friendly policies up to a point, and some have a track record of partnership working in Wales. Innovative solutions can be found which suit employers, employees and those in need of care. However, many of these schemes simply help women to participate in paid work: they do not address the issue of training, promotion and low pay.

So, after twenty years of equality legislation and dramatic industrial restructuring, more women may have taken up paid work but they appear still to have the major responsibility for domestic work and childcare. There can only be winners in the provision of high-quality, affordable childcare, family-friendly policies and a better balance between home and work for all.

6 Conclusion

Has there been progress in equal opportunities between men and women in Wales since the 1970s? The impact of the legislation has raised awareness and publicity surrounding the legal cases has brought attention to the fact that, in matters of pay, recruitment and promotion, it is illegal to discriminate on the grounds of gender. Positive-action measures have provided opportunities for women to overcome their disadvantages. On the other hand there is still a substantial pay gap between men and women, there are clear gender divisions in education, training and employment, and the lack of childcare facilities and uneven domestic division of labour has resulted in a female workforce in Wales whose skills, potential and qualifications are underused. There is clearly still work to be done if women's life-chances are not to be restricted by their gender and the Welsh economy is not to continue to be hampered by the under-utilization of women.

Many of the more obvious barriers have been removed but cultural, organizational and attitudinal obstacles remain. The long-hours culture, the uneven domestic division of labour, the devaluing of work undertaken on a part-time basis and the limited number of employers offering family-friendly policies are major problems. The lack of women in managerial and decision-making positions reinforces the status quo. With few women in senior positions, men and women lack experience of powerful, competent women. For women this means no role models or female mentors or networks. For men it reduces the confidence they have in appointing women to senior posts or channelling them into jobs where they will gain the experience essential for promotion. Gender-segregation patterns are astonishingly rigid in Wales, and in many sectors such as education and local government, the position of women appears to be worsening rather than improving.

The last two decades have been highly significant for women in the workforce in Wales. Participation has increased and part-time women workers now make up a quarter of the Welsh workforce. However, attitudes, culture and organizations will need to change dramatically before gender ceases to be the most significant determinant of who gets what job, what training and what pay. If women are to earn the same as men for their efforts, and if the economy is to be competitive by making full use of its human resources, we will have to mainstream the equality issue into all policies and practices here in Wales. This is a major step but a vital one if significant progress is to be achieved over the next two and a half decades.

Models of equal opportunities

It is possible to characterize three distinct approaches to equal opportunities in Wales over the last three decades. The first is the equal treatment approach, which was enshrined in the legislation in the 1970s with which this review begins. The major driver for the Sex Discrimination Act and the Equal Pay Act was the UK's aspiration to join and remain a member of the European Community: in order to satisfy entry requirements, the UK had to conform to the EC's Directives on equal treatment of men and women. The law is, however, a necessary but blunt instrument in tackling equality. Cases can take a considerable length of time and make personal and financial demands upon plaintiffs; they often do not reach court, and if they do, rarely result in a victory (Gregory 1989). Even victories do not necessarily lead to a satisfactory outcome, despite the removal of upper compensation limits during the 1990s which meant that to be found outside the law became more financially punitive and less worth the risk (Leonard 1987). The equal pay legislation has not resulted in equal pay, but merely removed some of the grosser and more visible forms of pay inequality.

This is not to say that equal treatment in the law is not essential: it clearly is. We cannot estimate its preventative effect. However, in Wales in particular, the record on cases taken to tribunals is disappointing. Members of Employment Tribunals do not receive training in discrimination and may decide that an employer has acted 'reasonably' (for example on sacking an employee who becomes pregnant) without understanding the complexity of the concept of discrimination, especially indirect discrimination. The lack of major private sector employers in Wales that have developed good practice in employment to act as a model for smaller companies is keenly felt. The public sector has historically been a good employer for women in

Wales, but there is little evidence of women reaching positions of senior management.

The equal treatment approach is clearly essential but it is predicated on the notion of treating men and women the same. However, they are not the same. There are significant differences in career trajectories, and it is the typical male pattern that is taken as the norm. Equal treatment, therefore, is translated as treating women the same as men.

The second approach to equal opportunities that can be detected is one where the shortcomings of equal treatment are recognized, and attempts are made to address the disadvantages women face in education, training and the labour market through a series of positive-action measures. The various initiatives such as the women-only workshops in the 1980s can be seen as falling into this category. These projects seek to focus attention on the 'special' needs of women and assist them to fit into existing systems. These projects have been exemplary, indeed some have become identified as model projects in the EU. They have been emulated elsewhere in the UK and abroad. Inevitably, however, they face difficulties. Their funding is precarious. They remain outside mainstream provision: indeed that is their strength. They can attract women for whom mainstream provision is inappropriate or in some way found wanting. They provide women-friendly opportunities. Their success in assisting highly disadvantaged women to return to learning, to take qualifications, to regain confidence and rejoin the labour market is rooted in their women-centred approach. There is much to be learnt from these examples by those currently concerned with delivering lifelong learning policies.

Positive action, however, can come with a health warning. While the focus is on the needs of women, the aim is to help equip them to adapt to and cope with the world the way it is. This is clearly necessary work, but it leaves the *modus vivendi* of mainstream organizations unchallenged. At one end of the continuum of such projects are training courses for women in middle management, grooming them for senior positions. The curriculum of such courses includes 'developing a killer instinct'; 'coping with the office romeo'; 'getting yourself heard in meetings' (Rees 1992). It is a particular version of management that is on offer. Such courses can, somewhat cynically, be regarded as remedial courses for women in how to behave more like a man! In this situation, employers who are able to promote such women into senior positions may feel that they have achieved their 'short agenda' (Cockburn 1989) of equal opportunities, but there is little change in the everyday lives and prospects of the majority of women employees. Moreover, there is a toll for such women, as Marshall (1995) shows. Conforming to patterns of behaviour and styles of management designed by male incumbents to suit their way of life, which includes presenteeism and long hours, can create such stress that highfliers choose to drop out.

Positive action is essential, to learn appropriate ways of delivering services, and organizing work. But it is not sufficient. The long battle to provide refuges for women and their children experiencing domestic violence in Wales has been vital work over the last twenty years. It has been extremely difficult to secure funding (Charles 1992) and to provide support and services in refuges appropriate for the diverse cultures within Wales (Charles and Davies 1997). Nevertheless, no one would argue that such refuges are the solution to domestic violence. Similarly, women-only training projects are but one ingredient within what needs to be a co-ordinated approach to developing equal opportunities in education, training and work.

The third phase towards equal opportunities, and one which characterizes the 1990s, is mainstreaming equality. It begins with the collection of baseline statistics so that the nature and shape of gender inequality within an organization or field of activity can be made familiar to all concerned. It needs to be followed up with the implementation of gender-monitoring statistics. The difficulties experienced in collecting and analysing gender-disaggregated statistics for the purposes of this review are evidence both of how much more organizations need to do to be in a position provide such statistics routinely, but also of how much progress there has been in this regard over the last twenty-five years. Building on the provision of such statistics, mainstreaming then involves the integration of gender equality into all policies, programmes and actions.

These three phases of equal treatment, positive action and mainstreaming, as accumulated fashions in equal opportunities policies are not, of course, unique to Wales. They are manifestations of broader trends which can be observed at a European level (Rees 1998). Indeed, European legislation has been one of the drivers of changes in Wales (see Landmarks section), and the availability of European funding for positive-action measures has facilitated many projects that have benefited women, levering resources from within Wales as matched funding which might not otherwise have been made available.

There are various landmarks that can be observed in the EU in the journey towards mainstreaming. The European Commission produced a Communication to the Council of Ministers advocating incorporating equal opportunities into all Community policies programmes and actions in 1996 (known as the mainstreaming communication) (Commission of the European Communities 1996). It produced its first annual report on equal opportunities between men and women in the European Union as a contribution to the mainstreaming agenda the following year (EC 1997). A committee of Commissioners chaired by President Jacques Santer is reviewing equal opportunities throughout the Commission, exploring how the individual Directorate Generals are performing on this issue. Monika Wulf Matheis, the Regional Affairs Commissioner, used a visit to Newport to declare publicly that she would not fund any bids for regional development projects that had not integrated equal opportunities into the bids (Chwarae Teg 1997b). Chwarae Teg has since been awarded Technical Assistance monies to assist bids for Structural Funds from Wales to integrate equality into their proposals (Chwarae Teg 1998). This is a pilot exercise which if successful may well spread throughout the EU. It is prompted in part by the fact that even those individuals who are aware of gender inequalities may not know how to address the issue in project design, monitoring and evaluation.

Attention to equal opportunities within the Commission and within those organizations keen to have their activities supported by the EU is of course patchy. The lack of expertise in mainstreaming is another issue. Here, it is mainstreaming which has a health warning. There is inevitably a concern that the mainstreaming approach will be used as an excuse to abandon all positive-action projects and programmes. If equal opportunities is being integrated, the argument runs, there is surely no need for 'special projects' for women. Indeed, the Equal Opportunities Unit of the European Commission has abolished some women's networks in the name of mainstreaming.

This is clearly a danger. It has to be recognized that mainstreaming is a long-term strategy. It needs to be developed alongside equal treatment approaches and build on an enhanced programme of positive action from which good practice can be developed and integrated into mainstream provision.

Initiatives taken by the EOC in Wales, such as the Equality Exchange, developing alliances with employers, trade unions, further and higher education providers and setting up Chwarae Teg in the early 1990s can be seen as developing a mainstreaming approach. Chwarae Teg and Opportunity 2000 are examples of partnership working. Rather than focusing on women, they turn their attention to employers seeking to persuade them to change their practices to become more women-friendly and inclusive. They tackle essential issues of organizational culture and practice. Their strength, like that of the EOC in Wales, lies in their partnership work.

The WDA, while not known generally for its work on gender equality, has played a crucial role through its contribution to Chwarae Teg, its research (Rees and Willox 1991a and 1991b) and its focus on women in its European collaborative partnership projects such as Athena, Axia and Diva (described in chapter 4). It will be crucial to ensure that gender equality is firmly embedded in the procedures and thinking of the new Economic Powerhouse for Wales and that these kinds of projects continue to draw attention to how organizations can be more gender-sensitive in their employment practices and delivery of services.

The EOC has adopted mainstreaming as its main strategic approach to the fostering of equal opportunities between women and men (EOC 1997b). It co-ordinated a project, in the EC's Fourth Medium Term Action Programme on Equal Opportunities for Women and Men on mainstreaming equality in local government. Two Welsh authorities participated in this project which sought to mainstream equality not simply into employment and recruitment practices but into the all-important and much neglected area of service delivery. It was precisely to address the needs of hidden voices, such as those articulated through the EOC's work with Black and ethnic minority women in Wales (EOC 1993; Baruah 1997) that this focus was adopted. The project led to the development of a framework for mainstreaming equality in local authorities, informed by the experience of the Welsh authorities, together with authorities in England, Scotland, Sweden, Italy and Ireland (EOC 1998).

As this review has shown, women in Wales are less likely to be in the labour market, have fewer vocational qualifications and earn less than women elsewhere in Britain and than men in Wales who themselves have low economic activity rates, poor qualifications and low pay. What can mainstreaming offer women in Wales? Indeed, what is mainstreaming?

Mainstreaming

Ultimately mainstreaming is the integration of equal opportunities in all policies, procedures, processes and indeed thinking about policy on both internal matters and service delivery and product manufacture. It can be described as a paradigm shift in thinking. It means finding out about the ways in which current systems and ways of doing things are not, as is commonly thought, gender-neutral, but in fact favour one or other gender (usually men). Gathering statistics and 'soft information' in the form of studies on a regular basis is the first step in developing awareness. Gender audits are now carried out regularly by some organizations. In Scotland, Brown et al. (1994) have begun the process. In Ireland, a collection of research studies from North and South has begun the process of collecting experiences (Byrne and Leonard 1997). In Wales, this review will hopefully contribute to the process by providing some indication of how far we have travelled and what the main issues are in achieving gender equality.

Gender monitoring illustrates that the equal access approach does not necessarily produce an equal outcome. Gender has a profound effect on patterns of distribution in education, training and employment. Moreover, there are of course differences among women and among men. We all have multiple identities and the particular mix of characteristics we have impacts upon the extent to which equal access is a reality. This was shown to an extent in Aaron et al. (1994) where we heard testaments from a woman who is both Welsh-speaking and a lesbian, but in whose life these two worlds are divided (Crwydren 1994); from a woman who in the same week as winning the prized Eisteddfod chair was imprisoned for being a political activist burning down second homes (Tomos 1994), and from a committed Christian deacon, denied by her Church the opportunity of being ordained in Wales (a ban since rescinded) (Morgan 1994). In the same way, there is increasing awareness that differences *among* the estimated 40,500 adults from ethnic minorities (Singh 1998) defy any generalization save the significant common experience of being regarded as 'other'. As Charlotte Williams, the daughter of a white Welsh-speaking woman and a black Guyanese father, writes:

> You have to fight to be black and you have to fight to be Welsh. As a black person the pride, value and authenticity of your experience are challenged

> by . . . neglect and racism. As a Welsh person, access to your Welsh self is countered by skin colour and the thousand little acts of social closure. It is difficult to think of yourself as Welsh when those around you with seemingly better credentials refuse to acknowledge your identity and yet continually challenge your black identity: 'Well you're not really black are you'. It's difficult to be black if you are starved of references to your heritage and to grow up in a land where there is no conception of black Welsh.
> (Williams 1997: 30)

Multiple identities mean that approaches to equal opportunities need to move beyond gender equality, and address other forms of discrimination and disadvantage more effectively, too. The differences among ethnic minorities are often ill-understood. While unemployment among some groups, such as Somalis in Cardiff, is extremely high, there have been notable successes among other groups in education and employment. Similarly, some 57 per cent of families in Wales include a disabled member (John 1998), yet the nature and combination of those disabilities vary enormously in terms of their implications. While being aware of diversity and the various permutations of equality dimensions in individuals and groups, we nevertheless need to acknowledge and respond to the clear patterns of disadvantage which monitoring can reveal to us. Shared disadvantages need to be addressed. Identifying and addressing systematic biases in the distribution of resources, opportunities and realities are essential elements of the mainstreaming agenda.

'Visioning' or seeing is necessary to understand how these systematic biases reproduce advantage and disadvantage. Privileging seniority as a criterion for promotion, for example, automatically disadvantages women who take career breaks. The language of the university, with its masters' and bachelors' degrees, says something to women about its openness to them. The lack of attention to the religious holidays of 'other' religions also sends messages. The gendering of the Welsh language in job adverts tells women Welsh-speakers whether they are deemed suitable or not for particular posts (Awbery 1997). The lack of disabled access, or colour-coded corridors for the visually impaired or feedback loops for the aurally impaired again indicates the dominant norm of able-bodiedness into which people are expected to fit. Visioning entails imagining other ways of organizing and doing. It entails having and realizing aspirations, building upon the experiences of positive action and consultative exercises.

The mainstreaming agenda is ambitious and means rethinking how we organize our institutions. The issue of equal opportunities is highly complex and inevitably means going beyond gender equality to accommodate difference and diversity. It is full of contradictions and is regarded by some as a dangerous area. Hence, it can be used as a cost-cutting exercise to abandon hard-won corners and concessions such as equality officers and units and women-only events and provision. Awareness-raising and training are essential to convey the concept. Building ownership is vital. Even then, mainstreaming is vulnerable to economic and political imperatives, and the new agendas of cultural change.

Nevertheless, if, in the next twenty-five years, gender is to have less of an impact on how resources and positions and opportunities are allocated, then the mainstreaming agenda needs to be pursued vigorously, in tandem with equal-treatment legislation and positive-action measures. In Wales it is clear that gender has more of an impact on life-chances than elsewhere in Britain. It is even more vital, therefore, that partnership initiatives within and beyond Wales are fostered by the EOC and Chwarae Teg and that others flourish and develop. More research is needed to chart 'progress' and aid understanding of the nature and complexities of gender relations and transformations. More training and awareness raising is needed to help us get to grips with the complexity of delivering equal opportunities. Then, we hope, there will be a more promising story to tell of equality for men and women in the next twenty-five years than there has been in the last.

Endnotes

1. There are two other sources worth mentioning here. The first is the CD-ROM produced by the Centre for Advanced Social Studies at University of Wales, Cardiff, which summarizes published and unpublished material on Wales. The second is a database of statistical and documentary material on *The Welsh Economy and Society Post-1945* produced by Dennis Thomas and Dot Jones and published by the University of Wales Press (1966). The database includes official publications and reports, books, newspapers, theses and statistics.
2. The economic activity rates are defined here as the proportion of women of working age (sixteen to sixty) either in employment or registered as unemployed (latterly – a jobseeker).
3. As Walby (1997: 32), drawing on the *New Earnings Survey*, comments for Britain: 'Part-time women earned only 60% of men's full-time hourly rates in 1995, and even this is an underestimate of part-time women's wages since the *New Earnings Survey* does not include the earnings of those beneath the PAYE tax threshold, which are estimated to involve one fifth of part-time workers . . .'
4. Unfortunately it is not possible to give a comparison with 1970 as the data are not available.
5. At the request of the EOC, the editor of the *Wales Yearbook*, sponsored annually by HTV, now gives a gender breakdown of members of Parliament, local authority councillors and chief officers and major public appointments in Wales (see Balsom 1997).
6. The EOC's annual factcard *Facts about Women and Men in Wales* provides one regular source of gender-disaggregated statistics (there are similar cards for Britain and Scotland), and the *Briefings on Men and Women in Britain* produced in 1997 give more detailed analysis on a series of topics. The Welsh Office has just published *Women: A Statistical Focus on Wales* (1998c) which provides for the first time gender-disaggregated data for Wales on a range of issues.

7. The EOC, Welsh Development Agency and Institute of Welsh Affairs commissioned research on women in senior management in Wales in 1998 to explore these factors: results should be available by early 1999.

Landmarks

1970	Sex Discrimination Act and Equal Pay Act is passed by Parliament Conservative Party wins general election Formation of Gay Liberation Front
1971	Mudiad Ysgolion Meithrin (Welsh-language nursery school movement) set up Immigration Act 1971 effectively stops black immigration except for wives and dependants 20.9 per cent of population in Wales claim to speak Welsh (1971 Census)
1973	UK becomes member of European Economic Community
1974	Local government reorganization
1975	EC Equal Pay Directive UK membership of EEC is confirmed by referendum Sex Discrimination Act and Equal Pay Act come into effect Equal Opportunities Commission set up Labour Party wins two general elections First refuge for battered women set up in Wales
1976	EC Equal Treatment Directive Chronically Sick and Disabled Persons Act (amended) allows equal access for disabled Race Relations Act outlaws direct and indirect discrimination on grounds of race, and sets up Commission for Racial Equality
1978	EOC office in Wales opens Welsh Women's Aid is established
1979	EC Social Security Directive Conservatives win general election Devolution referendum produces 'No' vote Establishment of Parliamentary Select Committee for Welsh Affairs

1981 British Nationality Act – eligibility to citizenship is effectively restricted to people born of UK parents or parents settled in UK
18.9 per cent of population in Wales claim to speak Welsh (1981 Census)
Greenham Common peace camp is established following march by women from Wales

1982 First Community Action Programme on the Promotion of Equal Opportunities for Men and Women (1982–5)
Launch of Sianel Pedwar Cymru (S4C)

1983 Equal Pay for Work of Equal Value Act
Conservatives win general election
Wales Assembly of Women is founded

1984/5 Miners' strike and setting up of women's support groups

1984 Women's Advisory Council of the Wales TUC set up
Dove Workshop opens in Banwen
South Glamorgan Women's Workshop opens in Cardiff

1986 EC Equal Treatment of the Self-employed Directive
Second Community Action Programme on the Promotion of Equal Opportunities for Men and Women (1986–90)
Disabled Persons (Services, Consultation and Representation) Act

1987 Conservatives win general election
Honno, Welsh Women's Press, is founded

1988 Education Reform Act grants public sector higher education institutions university status, and introduces National Curriculum and Standard Assessment Tests
Immigration Act effectively revokes rights of dependants to join men who entered Britain before the 1971 Act
Stonewall, parliamentary lobby group for gays, set up
First M.Sc. in Women's Studies in Wales started at University of Wales, Cardiff
Red Flannel Films' production of *Mam* premièred in Treorchy

1989 Employment Act reduces exceptions allowed under Sex Discrimination Act, for example restricting hours women may work

1989–1991 Seven Training and Enterprise Councils set up in Wales

1990 Last coal mine in Rhondda closes

1991 Third Community Action Programme on the Promotion of Equal Opportunities for Men and Women (1991–5)
Homeworkers' Bill
18.6 per cent of population in Wales claim to speak Welsh (1991 Census)
Responsibility for training passes to Welsh Office

1992 EC Pregnant Workers Directive
Conservatives win general election
Further and Higher Education Act grants colleges of further education incorporated status
Responsibility for higher education passes to Welsh Office
Chwarae Teg ('Fair Play') consortium launched
Opportunity 2000 launched in Wales
First all-Wales Black and Ethnic Minority Women's Conference is held, Cardiff

1993 Trade Union Reform and Employment Act makes dismissal of women for pregnancy unfair and enhances maternity rights. Additional entitlements for women with two years full-time or five years part-time continuous service
Welsh Language Act is passed, Welsh Language Board set up
Higher and Further Education Funding Councils for Wales set up
MEWN Cymru (Black and Ethnic Minority Women's Network) set up

1994 Age of consent for gays is lowered from 21 to 18 in Britain

1995 United Nations Fourth World Conference on Women, Beijing
Part-time workers are granted same employment protection rights as full-time workers
Disability Discrimination Act makes discrimination on grounds of disability unlawful for employers of twenty or more.
National Disability Council is established
Welsh Office launches *People and Prosperity: An Agenda for Action*

	Commission for Racial Equality opens office in Wales
1996	Twenty-one years of equality legislation in Britain EC Hours of Work Directive Fourth Community Action Programme on the Promotion of Equal Opportunities for Men and Women (1996–2000) EC Communication on Mainstreaming is published Employment Rights Act extends rights on maternity leave, pay and return to work Refugee and Asylum Seekers' Bill extends 'white list' of countries, restricts rights of refugees and asylum-seekers to social security benefits *In Pursuit of Equality in Wales: National Agenda for Action Wales Programme* published (Wales Assembly of Women et al. 1996) Local government and health authority reorganization in Wales
1997	EC Part-time Working Directive EC Burden of Proof in Discrimination Directive First EC *Annual Report on Equal Opportunities for Women and Men in the EU* is published EU Amsterdam Summit extends equal treatment and promotes mainstreaming Labour Party wins general election Devolution referendum produces 'Yes' vote
1998	National Assembly for Wales Bill includes equality clauses EC Parental Leave Directive Disability Rights Commission is announced

Equal Opportunities Commissioners for Wales:

Mr John Beale	Dec 1975–Dec 1979
Dr Anne Robinson	Jan 1980–Dec 1985
Professor Gillian Powell	Feb 1986–July 1989
Ms Noreen Bray	Sept 1990–Dec 1995
Professor Teresa Rees	June 1996–

References

Aaron, J., Rees, T., Betts, S. and Vincentelli, M. (eds.) (1994) *Our Sisters' Land: The Changing Identities of Women in Wales*, Cardiff: University of Wales Press.

Adler, D. (1989) 'Struggling On', in *Planet: The Welsh Internationalist*, No. 77, 45–50.

Arnot, M., David, M. and Weiner, G. (1996) *Educational Reforms and Gender Equality in Schools*, Manchester: Equal Opportunities Commission.

Ashton, S. (1994a) 'The Farmer Needs a Wife: Farm Women in Wales', in J. Aaron et al. (eds.), *Our Sisters' Land: The Changing Identities of Women in Wales*, Cardiff: University of Wales Press, pp. 122–39.

Ashton, S. (1994b) 'Working Women and Childcare: Wales in the Nineties', in *Women, Wales and Europe – Special Issue of Equal Opportunities International*, Vol. 13, No. 3/4/5, 29–38.

Aull Davies, C. (1989) *Welsh Nationalism in the Twentieth Century: The Ethnic Option and the Modern State,* London: Praeger.

Awbery, G. (1997) *The Sex Discrimination Act and the Use of Welsh in the Workplace*, Manchester: Equal Opportunities Commission.

Bagihole, B. (1994) *Women, Work and Equal Opportunities*, Aldershot: Avebury.

Bagihole, B. (1997) *Equal Opportunities and Social Policy*, London: Macmillan.

Balsom, D. (1997) *The Wales Yearbook 1998*, Cardiff: HTV.

Baruah, M. (1997) *Making Voices Heard: Access to Services by Black and Ethnic Minority Women*, Cardiff: MEWN Cymru.

Beddoe, D. (1986) 'Images of Welsh Women', in T. Curtis (ed.), *Wales: The Imagined Nation*, Bridgend: Poetry Wales Press, pp. 227–38.

Beechey, V. and Perkins, T. (1987) *A Matter of Hours: Women, Part-time Work and the Labour Market*, Oxford: Polity.

Bellin, W., Osmond, J. and Reynolds, D. (1994) *Towards an Educational Policy for All*, Cardiff: Institute of Welsh Affairs.

Betts, S. (1994) 'The Changing Family in Wales', in J. Aaron et al. (eds.), *Our Sisters' Land: The Changing Identities of Women in Wales,* Cardiff: University of Wales Press, pp. 17–30.

Betts, S., Griffiths, M. and Knight, P. (1995) *A Study of Students in Higher Education who have passed through Access Course Routes in Wales*, Report to Welsh Office, Bangor: University of Wales, Bangor.

Brown, A., Breitenbach, E. and Myers, F. (1994) 'Equality Issues in Scotland: A Research Review', in *Research Discussion Series No. 7*, Manchester: Equal Opportunities Commission.

Byrne, A. and Leonard, M. (eds.) (1997) *Women in Irish Society: A Sociological Reader*, Belfast: Beyond the Pale Productions.

Campbell, B. (1993) *Goliath: Britain's Dangerous Places*, London: Methuen.

Careers Service Wales (1994) *Pupil Destination Statistics in Wales, 1993,* in co-operation with BP Chemicals Ltd., Cardiff: Careers Service in Wales.

Central Statistical Office (1987) *Regional Trends*, London: HMSO.

Central Statistical Office (1995) *Regional Trends*, London: HMSO.

Charles, N. (1992) 'Funding of Welsh Women's Aid', in *Planet: The Welsh Internationalist*, No. 96, 85–90.

Charles, N. and Davies, C. A. (1997) 'Contested Communities: The Refuge Movement and Cultural Identities in Wales', in *Sociological Review*, Vol. 45, No. 3, 416–36.

Chwarae Teg (1993) *Good Childcare, Better Business: A Guide to Childcare Initiatives in Wales*, Pontypridd: Chwarae Teg.

Chwarae Teg (1996a) *Welsh Office Childcare Demonstration Projects for the Under Fives, Progress Report, August–December 1995*, Cardiff: Chwarae Teg.

Chwarae Teg (1996b) *Welsh Office Childcare Demonstration Projects for the Under Fives, Progress Report, January–March 1996*, Cardiff: Chwarae Teg.

Chwarae Teg (1996c) *Balance: The Newsletter of Chwarae Teg and Opportunity 2000*, Issue 15, Cardiff: Chwarae Teg.

Chwarae Teg (1996d) *Maximising Potential: Guide to Innovative Training and Education Activities in Wales for Women*, Cardiff: Chwarae Teg.

Chwarae Teg (1996e) *New Ways to Work: Business Benefits of a Family Friendly Work Environment*, Cardiff: Chwarae Teg.

Chwarae Teg (1997a) *Chwarae Teg Five Years On: Annual Report and Accounts 1996/7*, Cardiff: Chwarae Teg.

Chwarae Teg (1997b) *Women, Players in Regional Development Conference Report*, Cardiff: Chwarae Teg.

Chwarae Teg (1998) *Integrating Equal Opportunities in the Structural Funds*, Cardiff: Chwarae Teg.

Chwarae Teg and Carers National Association in Wales (1996) *Carers in Work: A Guide for Employers and Carers*, Cardiff: Chwarae Teg.

Cockburn, C. (1989) 'EO: The Long and Short Agenda', in *Industrial Relations Journal*, Vol. 20, No. 3, 213–25.

Commission of the European Communities (1996) *Incorporating Equal Opportunities for Women and Men into all Community Policies and Activities*, Communication from the Commission COM(96) 67 (final),

Luxembourg: Office for Official Publications of the European Communities.
Court, G. (1995) *Women in the Labour Market: Two Decades of Change and Continuity*, Report No. 294, Brighton: Institute for Employment Studies.
Crompton, R. and Sanderson, K. (1986) 'Credentials and Careers: Some Implications of the Increase in Professional Qualifications among Women', *Sociology*, Vol. 20, No. 1, pp. 25–42.
Crwydren, R. (1994) 'Welsh Lesbian Feminist: A Contradiction in Terms?', in J. Aaron et al. (eds.), *Our Sisters' Land: The Changing Identities of Women in Wales*, Cardiff: University of Wales Press, pp. 294–300.
Daniel, P. (1994) 'Promoting Gender Equality in Schools', in J. Aaron et al. (eds.), *Our Sisters' Land: The Changing Identities of Women in Wales*, Cardiff: University of Wales Press, pp. 161–80.
Davies, J. (1995) 'The Welsh Language', in T. Herbert and G. E. Jones (eds.), *Post-War Wales*, Cardiff: University of Wales Press, pp. 55–77.
Department for Education and Employment, Scottish Office and Welsh Office (1996) *Work and Family: Ideas and Options for Childcare*, London: DfEE/Scottish Office/Welsh Office.
EC Childcare Network (1996) *A Review of Services for Young Children in the European Union 1990–1995*, Brussels: Equal Opportunities Unit, DGV, European Commission.
Edwards, H. (1996) *Wales 1996: Land of Low Pay*, a Low Pay Unit Report presented at National Local Government Forum in Wales AGM and conference, Cwmbran, 17 May 1996.
Equal Opportunities Commission (1993) *Making Voices Heard – All Wales Black and Ethnic Minority Women's Conference Report*, Cardiff: Equal Opportunities Commission.
Equal Opportunities Commission (1997a) *Partnering Equality: Annual Report 1996*, Manchester: Equal Opportunities Commission.
Equal Opportunities Commission (1997b) *EOC Corporate Plan 1997–2001*, Manchester: Equal Opportunities Commission.
Equal Opportunities Commission (1998) *Mainstreaming Gender Equality in Local Government: A Framework*, Manchester: Equal Opportunities Commission.
Equal Opportunities Commission/Chwarae Teg (1993) *Realising Potential: Increasing the Effectiveness of Education and Training Provision for Women*, Cardiff: Equal Opportunities Commission.
ERES (1994) *A Study of the Economically Inactive and their Role in the Labour Market*, Report for the Welsh Office Statistics and Economics Divisions, Cardiff: ERES.
ERES (1996) *The Role of Women in the Welsh Workforce: Final Report for Chwarae Teg*, Cardiff: ERES.

Essex, S., Callender, C., Rees, T. and Winckler, V. (1986) *New Styles of Training for Women: An Evaluation of South Glamorgan Women's Workshop*, Manchester: Equal Opportunities Commission.
European Commission (1994) *European Social Policy: A Way Forward for the Union*, Luxembourg: Office for Official Publications of the European Communities.
European Commission (1997) *Annual Report from the Commission: Equal Opportunities for Women and Men in the European Union*, COM(96) 650 (final), Luxembourg: Office for Official Publications of the European Communities.
Felstead, A. (1996a) 'Homeworking in Britain: The National Picture in the Mid-1990s', in *Industrial Relations Journal*, Vol. 27, No. 3, 225–38.
Felstead, A. (1996b) 'Gender Inequalities in the Distribution of Vocational Qualifications', in *Gender, Work and Organisation*, Vol. 3, No. 1, 38–50.
Francis, H., Rees, G. and Reid, S. (1996) *Gender and Participation in Adult Continuing Education*, Swansea: Department of Adult Continuing Education, University of Wales, Swansea.
Garland, P. (1992) *North Wales Access Consortium Research Project*, Bangor: University College of North Wales Bangor.
Garland, P. (1994) 'Educating Rhian: Experiences of Mature Women Students in North Wales', in J. Aaron et al. (eds.), *Our Sisters' Land: The Changing Identities of Women in Wales*, Cardiff: University of Wales Press, pp. 107–21.
Gershuny, J., Miles, I., Jones, S., Mullings, C., Thomas, G. and Wyatt, S. (1986) 'Time Budgets: Preliminary Analyses of a National Survey', in *Quarterly Journal of Social Affairs*, Vol. 2, No. 1, 13–39.
Gregory, J. (1989) *Trial by Ordeal: A Study of People who Lost Equal Pay and Sex Discrimination Cases in Industrial Tribunals,* Manchester: Equal Opportunities Commission.
Griffiths, M. (1992) *North Wales Access to Higher Education Students: Who Are They? Where are 'the Cymry'?*, Wales Access Unit, North Wales Access Consortium.
Hanney, M., Holterman, S. and Stone, M. (1993) *An Audit of Childcare in Wales*, Treforest: Chwarae Teg/Early Childhood Unit (Wales) of the National Children's Bureau.
Hansard Society Commission on Women at the Top (1990) *The Report of the Hansard Society Commission on Women at the Top*, London: Hansard Society Commission on Women at the Top.
Herbert, T. and Jones, G. E. (eds.) (1995) *Post-War Wales*, Cardiff: University of Wales Press.
Humphries, J. and Rubery, J. (eds.) (1996) *The Economics of Equal Opportunities*, Manchester: Equal Opportunities Commission.
Hutton, W. (1995) *The State We're In*, London: Jonathan Cape.

Istance, D. and Rees, T. (1994) *Women in Post Compulsory Education and Training in Wales*, Manchester: Equal Opportunities Commission.

Istance, D. and Rees, G. (1995) *Lifelong Learning in Wales: A Programme for Prosperity: A NIACE Cymru Policy Discussion Document*, Cardiff: NIACE Cymru.

Istance, D. and Rees, T. (1996) 'Escaping the Low Wage/Low Skill Syndrome: The Case for Investing in Women's Skills', *British Journal of Education and Work*, Vol. 9, No. 1, 43–58.

Istance, D., Rees, G., and Williamson, H. (1994) *Young People not in Education, Training or Employment in South Glamorgan*, Cardiff: South Glamorgan TEC and UWCC Cardiff.

Jenkins, R. and Hutson, S. (1990) 'Gender Relations, Family Relations and Long Term Youth Unemployment', in C. C. Harris (ed.), *Family, Economy and Community*, Cardiff: University of Wales Press.

John, A. (1984) *By the Sweat of their Brow: Women Workers at the Victorian Coal Mines*, London: Routledge and Kegan Paul.

John, H. (1998) 'The Welsh Labour Market: Equal Opportunities Imperatives', in Chwarae Teg, *Integrating Equal Opportunities in the Structural Funds*, Cardiff: Chwarae Teg.

Jones, H.M. (1993) 'A Survey of the Welsh Language: the 1992 Welsh Social Survey', *Statistical News*, Vol. 102, London: HMSO.

Leonard, A. (1987) *Pyrrhic Victories: Winning Sex Discrimination and Equal Pay Cases in the Industrial Tribunals 1980–84*, London: HMSO.

Leonard, D. (1980) *Sex and Generation: A Study of Courtship and Weddings*, London: Tavistock.

Levitas, R. and Guy, W. (eds.) (1996) *Interpreting Official Statistics*, London: Routledge.

Lodge, P., Parry-Langdon, N., and Fielder, S. (1991) *The Experience of Access Course Students Proceeding to Selected Higher Education Institutions in Wales*, Cardiff: Wales Access Unit and School of Social and Administrative Studies, University of Wales, Cardiff.

MacNamara, F. (1990) 'Women and Training', University of Wales College of Cardiff M.Sc. Econ. in Women's Studies, unpublished dissertation.

Marsh, C. (1991) *Hours of Women and Men in Britain*, Equal Opportunities Research Series, London: HMSO.

Marshall, J. (1995) *Women Managers Moving On: Exploring Career and Life Choices*, London: Routledge.

Martin, J. and Roberts, C. (1984) *Women and Employment Survey: A Lifetime Perspective*, London: HMSO.

McGiveney, V. (1994) *Wasted Potential: Training and Career Progression for Part-time and Temporary Workers*, Leicester: NIACE (National Organisation for Adult Learning).

McRae, S. (1996) 'Women at the Top: Progress after Five Years, a follow up report to the Hansard Society Commission on Women at the Top', *King Hall Paper No. 2*, London: Hansard Society.

Morgan, E. (1994) 'Identity and Religion', in J. Aaron et al. (eds.), *Our Sisters' Land: The Changing Identities of Women in Wales*, Cardiff: University of Wales Press, pp. 267–72.

Morgan, E. (1995) 'Women in Welsh Society', BBC Annual Radio Lecture, Cardiff: BBC.

Morgan, K. and Roberts, E. (1993) 'The Democratic Deficit: A Guide to Quangoland', *Papers in Planning Research*, No. 144, Cardiff: Dept. of City and Regional Planning, University of Wales, Cardiff.

Muir, E. J. (1994) 'The Highest Honour', in J. Aaron et al. (eds.), *Our Sisters' Land: The Changing Identities of Women in Wales*, Cardiff: University of Wales Press, pp. 301–7.

National Local Government Forum Against Poverty (1996) *Indicators of Poverty: Welsh Unitary Authorities*, Cardiff: Economic Research and Information, South Glamorgan County Council.

NHS Cymru (1993) *Understanding Flexibility: A Guide to Flexible Work Practices*, Llanelli: Chwarae Teg.

Office for National Statistics (1994) *Labour Force Survey*, London: HMSO.

Office for National Statistics (1995) *Labour Force Survey*, London: HMSO.

Office for National Statistics (1998) *Social Trends 28*, London: Stationery Office.

Office of Population, Censuses and Surveys (OPCS) (1994) *1991 Census: Wales*, London: HMSO.

Opportunity 2000 (1994) 'International Year of the Family', in *Opportunity 2000 Quarterly Update*, Autumn.

Opportunity 2000 (1996) *Women in Management: A Vital Resource for Wales*, Cardiff: Opportunity 2000.

Owen, D. (1994) *Ethnic Minority Women and the Labour Market: Tables Derived from the 1991 Census*, Manchester: Equal Opportunities Commission.

Park, A. (1994) *England and Wales Youth Cohort Study – Cohort 4: Young People 18–19 years old. Report on Sweep 3*, Youth Cohort Series No. 29, Sheffield: Employment Department.

Phizacklea, A. and Wolkowitz, C. (1995) *Homeworking Women: Gender, Racism and Class at Work*, London: Sage.

Piachaud, D. (1985) *Round about 50 Hours a Week*, London: Child Poverty Action Group.

Pilcher, J. (1994) 'Who Should Do the Dishes? Three Generations of Welsh Women Talking about Men and Housework', in J. Aaron et al. (eds.), *Our Sisters' Land: The Changing Identities of Women in Wales*, Cardiff: University of Wales Press, pp. 31–47.

Pilcher, J., Delamont, S., Powell, G. and Rees, T. (1988) 'The Women's Training Roadshow and the 'Manipulation' of Schoolgirls' Career Choices', in *British Journal of Education and Work*, Vol. 2, No. 2, 61–6.

Pilcher, J., Delamont, S., Powell, G., Rees, T. and Read, M. (1989a) 'Evaluating a Careers Convention: methods, results and implications', in *Research Papers in Education*, Vol. 4, No. 1, 57–76.

Pilcher, J., Delamont, S., Powell, G. and Rees, T. (1989b) 'Challenging Occupational Stereotypes: Women's Training Roadshows and Guidance at School Level', in *British Journal of Guidance and Counselling*, Vol. 17, No. 1, 59–67.

Pilcher, J., Delamont, S., Powell, G., Rees, T. and Read, M. (1990) *An Evaluative Study of Cardiff Women's Training Roadshow*, Cardiff: Welsh Office.

Pudner, H. and Francis, M. (1994) 'Women in the Workforce: Alternative Choices for Women in Coal-mining Areas', in *Women, Wales and Europe – Special Issue of Equal Opportunities International*, Vol. 13, No. 3/4/5, 50–61.

Rees, C. and Willox, I. (1991a) *Expanding the Role of Women in the South Wales Workforce*, Cardiff: Welsh Development Agency.

Rees, C. and Willox, I. (1991b) 'A Survey of Women's Experiences and Perceptions of the South Wales Labour Market', Research programme on Expanding the Role of Women in the South Wales Workforce, Cardiff: Welsh Development Agency.

Rees, G. and Fielder, S. (1992) 'The Services Economy, Sub-contracting and New Employment Relations: Contract Catering and Cleaning', in *Work, Employment and Society*, Vol. 6, No. 2, 347–68.

Rees, G. and Rees, T. (1980) 'Educational Inequality in Wales: Some Problems and Paradoxes', in G. Rees and T. Rees (eds.), *Poverty and Social Inequality in Wales*, London: Croom Helm, pp. 71–92.

Rees, G. and Thomas, M. (1991) 'From Coalminers to Entrepreneurs? A Case Study in the Sociology of Reindustrialization', in M. Cross and G. Payne (eds.), *Work and the Enterprise Culture*, Lewes: Falmer, pp. 57–78.

Rees, G., Williamson, H. and Istance, D. (1996) ' "Status Zero": A Study of Jobless School-leavers in South Wales', in *Research Papers in Education*, Vol. 11, No. 2, 219–35.

Rees, T. (1992) *Women and the Labour Market*, London: Routledge.

Rees, T. (1993) 'Women's Training Workshops in New Information Technologies', in *International Journal of Community Education*, Vol. 1, No. 4, 22–5.

Rees, T. (1994a) 'Women and Paid Work', in J. Aaron et al. (eds.), *Our Sisters' Land: The Changing Identities of Women in Wales*, Cardiff: University of Wales Press, pp. 89–106.

Rees, T. (1994b) 'Information Technology Skills and Access to Training

Opportunities: Germany and the UK', in K. Ducatel (ed.), *Employment and Technical Change in Europe: Work Organization, Skills and Training*, London: Edward Arnold, pp. 113–35.

Rees, T. (1994c) *ATHENA: Skills, Training and Women's Economic Development*, Report of a Conference held in Ewloe, North Wales, Pontypridd: Gateway Europe, Welsh Development Agency.

Rees, T. (1994d) *Women Employees' Training Needs in Wales, Catalonia, Dublin and Thessaloniki: Axia Project Synthesis Report*, Pontypridd: Gateway Europe, Welsh Development Agency.

Rees, T. (1994e) 'Feminising the Mainstream: Women and the EC Training Programmes', in *Equal Opportunities International*, Vol. 13, No. 3/4/5, 9–28.

Rees, T. (1995a) *Axia: Revitalising Companies by Realising Women's Economic Potential*, Cardiff: Gateway Europe, Welsh Development Agency.

Rees, T. (1995b) 'Women in Post-War Wales', in T. Herbert and G. E. Jones (eds.), *Post-War Wales*, Cardiff: University of Wales Press, pp. 78–106.

Rees, T. (1998) *Mainstreaming Equality in the European Union*, London: Routledge.

Rees, T. and Fielder, S. (1991) *Women and Top Jobs in Wales*, Report for HTV Wales, Cardiff: Social Research Unit, University of Wales College of Cardiff.

Rees, T. and Fielder, S. (1992) 'Smashing the Dark Glass Ceiling: Women and Top Jobs in Wales', in *Contemporary Wales: An Annual Review of Economic and Social Research*, Vol. 5, Cardiff: University of Wales Press, 99–114.

Reynolds, D. (1995) 'Creating an Educational System for Wales', in *Welsh Journal of Education*, Vol. 4, No. 2, 4–21.

Rubery, J., Smith, M., Fagan, C. and Grimshaw, D. (1998) *Women and European Employment*, London: Routledge.

Salisbury, J. (1994) 'Chasing Credentials: Women Further Education Teachers and In-service Training', in J. Aaron et al. (eds.), *Our Sisters' Land: The Changing Identities of Women in Wales*, Cardiff: University of Wales Press, pp. 140–60.

Salisbury, J. (1996a) *Educational Reforms and Gender Equality in Welsh Schools*, Manchester: Equal Opportunities Commission.

Salisbury, J. (1996b) 'Take Our Daughters to Work: A Positive Action For Some School Girls in Wales', in S. Betts (ed.), *Our Daughters' Land: Past and Present*, Cardiff: University of Wales Press, pp. 170–200.

Singh, R. (1998) 'The Welsh Labour Market: Equal Opportunities Imperatives', in Chwarae Teg, *Integrating Equal Opportunities in the Structural Funds*, Cardiff: Chwarae Teg, pp. 12–14.

Sly, F., Duxley, R. and Tillsley, C. (1995) 'Disability and the Labour

Market: Findings from the Labour Force Survey', in *Labour Market Trends*, London: Department for Education and Employment.

Smith, I. (1993) 'How Learned is my Valley: A Community University is Soon to Open in Welsh Mining Country', in *The Times*, 27 September.

Southall, J. (1990) 'Girls, Women and Occupational Choice', M.Sc. Econ. in Women's Studies dissertation, Cardiff: University of Wales.

Startup, R. and Dressel, B. M. (1996) 'The Culture and Aspirations of Welsh Secondary School Pupils: A Comparison Between the Sexes', in S. Betts (ed.), *Our Daughters' Land: Past and Present*, Cardiff: University of Wales Press, pp.127–46.

Stratham, J., Holterman, S. and Stone, M. (1996) *Childcare in Wales: The 1996 Audit*, Cardiff: Chwarae Teg.

Tomos, A. (1994) 'A Welsh Lady', in J. Aaron et al. (eds.), *Our Sisters' Land: The Changing Identities of Women in Wales*, Cardiff: University of Wales Press, pp. 259–66.

Venus, J. (1994) 'Playing an Active Role in Training Networks', in *Women, Wales and Europe – Special Issue of Equal Opportunities International*, Vol. 13, No. 3/4/5, 67–73.

Walby, S. (1997) *Gender Transformations*, London: Routledge.

Wales Assembly of Women, EOC, National Federation of Women's Institutes Wales, Welsh Women's Aid, Chwarae Teg, MEWN Cymru, Merched y Wawr and Wales Women's Euro Network (1996) *In Pursuit of Equality in Wales: National Agenda for Action Wales Programme*, London: Women's National Commission.

Wales TUC (1994) *Tackling the Low Pay, No Jobs Economy*, Cardiff: Wales TUC.

Walker, A. (1992) 'Women and the Organisation of the Labour Force in the Aberystwyth Hotel Trade', in *Contemporary Wales: An Annual Review of Economics and Social Research*, Vol. 5, Cardiff: University of Wales Press, pp. 131–64.

Welsh Development Agency (1993a) *Directory of Welsh Involvement in European Education, Training and Youth Programmes*, Pontypridd: Gateway Europe, Welsh Development Agency.

Welsh Development Agency (1993b) *Synthesis Report of the Athena Project*, Pontypridd: Gateway Europe, Welsh Development Agency.

Welsh Development Agency (1993c) *Women Entrepreneurs, Skills Training and Enterprise Development*, Report for Commission of the European Communities Task Force Human Resources Education Training and Youth.

Welsh Office (1993a) *Further and Higher Education and Training Statistics in Wales, No. 1, 1993*, Cardiff: Government Statistical Service.

Welsh Office (1993b) *People and Prosperity: A Challenge to Wales*, Cardiff: Welsh Office.

Welsh Office (1994a) *Welsh Economic Trends*, No. 15, Cardiff: Welsh Office.

Welsh Office (1994b) *Further and Higher Education and Training Statistics in Wales, No. 2, 1994*, Cardiff: Government Statistical Service.

Welsh Office (1994c) *Statistics of Education and Training in Wales: Schools, No. 2, 1994*, Cardiff: Welsh Office.

Welsh Office (1994d) *1992 Welsh Social Survey: Report on Education and Training*, Cardiff: Welsh Office.

Welsh Office (1994e) *Digest of Welsh Statistics No. 40, 1994*, Cardiff: Welsh Office.

Welsh Office (1995a) *1994/5 Welsh Training and Education Survey*, Cardiff: Welsh Office.

Welsh Office (1995b) *Welsh Economic Trends No. 16*, Cardiff: Welsh Office.

Welsh Office (1995c) *People and Prosperity: An Agenda for Action in Wales*, Cardiff: Welsh Office.

Welsh Office (1997) *Digest of Welsh Statistics 1997*, Cardiff: Welsh Office.

Welsh Office (1998a) *Statistics of Education and Training in Wales: Schools 1997*, Cardiff: Welsh Office.

Welsh Office (1998b) *Learning is for Everyone: The BEST for Lifelong Learning – A Welsh Office Green Paper*, Cardiff: Welsh Office.

Welsh Office (1998c) *Women: A Statistical Focus on Wales*, Cardiff: Welsh Office.

Wenger, C. (1994) 'Old Women in Rural Wales: Variations in Adaptations', in J. Aaron et al. (eds.), *Our Sisters' Land: The Changing Identities of Women in Wales*, Cardiff: University of Wales Press, pp. 61–85.

Williams, C. (1997) ' "Colour in the Pictures": Stories from a Childhood in Wales', in *Planet: The Welsh Internationalist*, No. 125, 25–30.

Willox, I. (1992) *Under-utilisation of Skills in North West Wales*, Pontypridd: Welsh Development Agency.

Women's National Commission, Equal Opportunities Commission, Equal Opportunities Commission for Northern Ireland (1996) *In Pursuit of Equality: A National Agenda for Action*, London: Women's National Commission.

Index